STORIES OF DAILY LIFE FROM
THE ROMAN WORLD

What did Roman children do first when they arrived at school in the morning? What excuse for missing school could be counted on to stave off a whipping from the teacher? What did a Roman banker do when someone came to borrow money? What did a Roman wife say when her husband came home drunk? The answers to such questions can be found not in mainstream ancient literature (whose writers had their minds on higher things) but in language textbooks for ancient Latin learners. These 'Colloquia' offer an ancient introduction to Roman culture, covering shopping, banking, bathing, dining, arguing, going to school, etc.; recently rediscovered, they are here presented for the first time in a format aimed at readers with no knowledge of Latin, Greek, or the ancient world. They come complete with introductory material, extensive illustrations, and a full explanation of their fascinating history.

ELEANOR DICKEY was educated at Bryn Mawr and Oxford, has taught in Canada and the United States, and is currently Professor of Classics at the University of Reading in England. She is a Fellow of the British Academy and has published more than 100 scholarly works, including *Greek Forms of Address* (1996), *Latin Forms of Address* (2002), *Ancient Greek Scholarship* (2007), *The Colloquia of the Hermeneumata Pseudodositheana* (2012–15), *Learning Latin the Ancient Way* (2016), *Introduction to the Composition and Analysis of Greek Prose* (2016), and *Learn Latin from the Romans* (2017). She is a dedicated and passionate teacher who enjoys introducing students to the ancient world and has brought decades of experience to making this book clear and accessible to people with no prior background in classics.

D0144138

STORIES OF DAILY LIFE FROM THE ROMAN WORLD

Extracts from the Ancient Colloquia

ELEANOR DICKEY

University of Reading

with illustrations by the author

CAMBRIDGE
UNIVERSITY PRESS

University Printing House, Cambridge CB2 8BS, United Kingdom

One Liberty Plaza, 20th Floor, New York, NY 10006, USA

477 Williamstown Road, Port Melbourne, VIC 3207, Australia

314–321, 3rd Floor, Plot 3, Splendor Forum, Jasola District Centre,
New Delhi – 110025, India

79 Anson Road, #06–04/06, Singapore 079906

Cambridge University Press is part of the University of Cambridge.

It furthers the University's mission by disseminating knowledge in the pursuit of
education, learning, and research at the highest international levels of excellence.

www.cambridge.org
Information on this title: www.cambridge.org/9781107176805
DOI: 10.1017/9781316817261

© Eleanor Dickey 2017

First published 2017
3rd printing 2019

Printed in the United Kingdom by TJ International Ltd. Padstow, Cornwall

A catalogue record for this publication is available from the British Library.

Library of Congress Cataloging-in-Publication Data
NAMES: Dickey, Eleanor, author.
TITLE: Stories of daily life from the Roman world : extracts from the ancient
Colloquia / Eleanor Dickey ; with illustrations by the author.
DESCRIPTION: Cambridge ; New York, NY : Cambridge University Press, 2017. |
Includes bibliographical references and index. |
IDENTIFIERS: LCCN 2017012388 | ISBN 9781107176805 (alk. paper)
SUBJECTS: LCSH: Rome – Social life and customs. | Conduct of life – Rome.
CLASSIFICATION: LCC DS272 .H47 2017 | DDC 937–dc23
LC record available at https://lccn.loc.gov/2017012388

ISBN 978-1-107-17680-5 Hardback
ISBN 978-1-316-62728-0 Paperback

Dedicated to

JUDY K. MORRIS

and

JONAS MORRIS

with gratitude for many decades of inspiration

Contents

Figures

Preface

The ancient Colloquia, a set of elementary language-learning materials from the Roman empire, contain fascinating information on many aspects of daily life in the Roman world, but they have long been neglected because until recently they had neither a modern edition nor a translation into any modern language. Most classicists have never heard of them, as indeed I had not until a few years ago. But as soon as I started working on these texts I fell in love with them; I felt they had tremendous potential and wanted everyone to be able to use them, a desire that led to production of a full scholarly edition of the Colloquia with translation and detailed commentary (Dickey 2012–15). That edition contains the arguments for the editorial and interpretive decisions underpinning the work presented here.

This book, by contrast, aims simply to present the Colloquia to non-specialist readers, people who would like to know what these texts tell us about ordinary life in the Roman empire and who are prepared to take my restoration and translation of the text on trust. Readers should be aware that alternative interpretations are often possible; note in particular that all words in italics are editorial additions, as are all speaker designations.

Because the Colloquia provide so much interesting information about daily life during the Roman empire, modern teachers may wish to use them as a cultural textbook, rather as ancient teachers did. For this purpose the Colloquia are only partly suitable, since many topics that we might expect to find in a well-rounded textbook on Roman civilisation are not mentioned in the Colloquia: love, marriage, agriculture, the army, and death, for example. But within their limitations, that is when combined with other sources that cover different topics, the Colloquia offer an excellent introduction to daily life during the empire. Therefore in designing this book I have tried to keep in mind both the needs of readers who would like to use the book as a general introduction to those aspects of Roman culture that the

Colloquia illuminate and readers whose main goal is to understand the Colloquia themselves.

Context for the Colloquia extracts presented here, therefore, is provided not only by the introductions to each passage and accompanying illustrations, but also by two additional chapters. The first of these (Chapter 11) includes parallel passages from other sources that readers might want to use alongside the Colloquia, selected on the basis of four criteria: that they be directly relevant to topics discussed in the Colloquia, roughly contemporary with the Colloquia, fun and interesting in their own right, and not from works that really ought to be read intact if one is interested in Roman daily life. For example, the letters of Cicero and Pliny, the novel of Petronius, the poems of Juvenal, and the plays of Plautus contain a good deal of information about daily life, and Quintilian's treatise on the education of an orator offers valuable insights into ancient education, but those are all works that can and should be read as wholes if one is interested in the topics they address; excerpts taken out of context would be inadequate to represent their contents and perhaps misleading. Indeed many people interested in daily life do read these texts separately and might well start with them rather than with the Colloquia, making extracts from them redundant here. The texts selected for use as parallels here are normally short; they include selections from the joke book of Philogelos, Vindolanda tablets, papyrus letters, inscriptions and graffiti, recipes from Apicius' cookbook, and poems of Martial. The final chapter offers a more detailed explanation of what the Colloquia are and how they were created, used, and transmitted to our time.

The illustrations are chosen on criteria similar to those governing the selection of parallel texts and aim to provide readers with images directly useful for understanding the Colloquia and the aspects of the Roman world to which they pertain. The illustrations are the visual equivalent of an ancient text in translation, in that they are all clear drawings of intact objects, immediately intelligible to the novice. Of course, many objects worth illustrating do not survive intact, and therefore the drawings sometimes show partial restorations (e.g. missing portions of a mosaic filled in when it is reasonably clear what they originally contained), modern reconstructions (e.g. the baths at the Xanten Archaeological Park), or artists' conceptions existing only on paper (e.g. Gismondi's drawing of Roman apartment buildings).

Restorations and reconstructions are signalled in the captions. Drawings rather than photographs are provided both because drawings are usually clearer and easier to understand than the type of photographs that can be included in a reasonably-priced book, and because partial restoration is much easier in a drawing. All the drawings are my own, though in some cases they are closely based on ones produced by earlier scholars (as acknowledged in the captions). These illustrations are no doubt less beautiful and evocative than photographs of ruins would be, just as a translation of a Latin poem is less beautiful and evocative than the original, but it is hoped that readers will find them clearer and more understandable to the same degree as a translation.

Restoration has its limits, however, just as translation does: it is important to be sure that one represents antiquity as it actually was, not as we like to think it was. For this reason one famous image does not appear in the chapter on ancient schooling; it can be found in the Appendix, with an explanation of why I do not think it belongs earlier in this book.

The choice of which aspects of the Colloquia to bring out in my explanatory text has been based on an assessment of which aspects of the information contained in the Colloquia are likely to be most useful and interesting to modern readers, given what other sources we already have about the ancient world. For example, although the Colloquia frequently mention food they are not really a good source for learning about ancient food, because we have many other ancient works that discuss food in far more depth; someone whose main goal is to learn about ancient food would not want to use the Colloquia as his or her first port of call. On the other hand the Colloquia are one of our best sources for information on ancient schools, not only because they say more about schools than about food, but also because other texts say less about schools: it would be entirely sensible to come first to the Colloquia when wanting to find out about ancient schools. I have accordingly focussed the explanatory material much more on topics for which the Colloquia represent an important resource than on topics for which they do not.

All translations are my own.

All dates are AD unless otherwise specified.

I am very grateful to Philomen Probert, Martin West, and Chia-Lin Hsu for reading drafts of this book and suggesting valuable corrections, and to John Peter Wild for advice about several of the illustrations; all these people also offered much-needed encouragement. Fergus Millar kindly offered a correction to my original translation of passage 3.2. Vincent Hunink, who translated the Colloquia into Dutch for publication as *In een Romeins klaslokaal* (Athenaeum, 2017), challenged my interpretations of a number of passages, resulting in some important improvements over my earlier translations of the Colloquia: I am extremely grateful for his thoughtful suggestions, even on points where we ultimately had to agree to disagree. Likewise Arian Verheij, who translated my English for the same volume, has significantly improved the work by his insightful corrections. I am also grateful to the Leverhulme Trust for generous funding that enabled me to finish this project, to Ineke Sluiter and the University of Leiden for providing excellent facilities in which to work on it, to the Arts and Humanities Research Council for the funding that enabled me to carry out the research on which it is ultimately based, to Rolando Ferri for introducing me to the Colloquia and helping me understand them, to Michael Sharp for patient encouragement over a long period, and to Marianna Prizio, Malcolm Todd, and Henry Maas of Cambridge University Press for their care, attention, and sharp-eyed intelligence.

CHAPTER I

Introduction

What did Roman children do first when they arrived at school in the morning? What did they bring with them? What excuse for missing school could be counted on to stave off a whipping from the teacher? What did a Roman banker do when someone came to borrow money? What did a grateful client say to his lawyer after winning a lawsuit? What did a Roman say if he needed to use the toilet? What had to be done before going to bed in a Roman household? These are not the types of questions for which the answers can be easily found in mainstream ancient literature, for Latin literature generally had its mind on higher things.

In the modern world, this kind of information about foreign cultures is often conveyed by language textbooks. A French textbook provides vignettes involving French people engaged in everyday activities in France, while a German textbook depicts German people in typical situations in Germany. Both alert foreign learners to cultural differences that may arouse interest, or that may cause foreigners difficulty if they are not forewarned. The same was true in antiquity, when Latin textbooks used little dialogues and narratives about Roman people engaged in everyday Roman activities both to teach useful Latin expressions and to inform Greek-speaking readers about Roman culture.

These dialogues and narratives, known as 'Colloquia', are the focus of this book: descriptions of the Roman world composed by people who knew it first-hand in order to help foreigners understand it. The Roman world was of course a large and varied one, both in time and in space, and the Colloquia range across it rather than focussing on a single period, since they were not written all at once by a single individual. Instead, they are a set of works adapted and expanded by teachers working at different times and places. Their oldest portions, the school scenes, go back at least to the first century AD and probably well into the Republic. The original version of these scenes was composed in a Latin-speaking area, probably Rome itself, to help Roman children learn Greek; it may have been used by Republican figures such as Julius Caesar, Cicero, or even earlier Romans when they were at school. The versions we have, however, are imperial-period adaptations and reworkings of that original. They provide a fascinating glimpse into the daily activities of schoolchildren – what they studied, how they studied, what they brought to school with them, how they squabbled when the teacher was not looking, etc. Because we have few other sources of information about schools, the school scenes are often considered to be the most important portions of the Colloquia.

The portions of the Colloquia describing the activities of adults, however, also offer many valuable glimpses into ancient society. They have a separate origin from the school scenes: the adult scenes were composed mostly in the second and third centuries AD, in the Greek-speaking Eastern empire, for the use of people learning Latin. Despite being written by and for residents of the Greek-speaking East, these portions of the textbooks consistently depict life in the Latin-speaking West, just as modern foreign-language textbooks reflect the culture of the language being taught rather than that of its learners. They tell a visitor how to negotiate a visit to a Roman public bath, how to borrow money, what to say at a dinner party, etc.

Unlike most modern language-teaching textbooks, the Colloquia are completely bilingual: every sentence in them appears both in Greek and in Latin. This dual presentation was the rule for elementary language instruction in antiquity, when differences in writing conventions made reading in a foreign language far more difficult than it is for modern students. It also made the Colloquia easy to transfer between one half of the empire and the other: the portions designed for Latin speakers learning Greek could be adapted for Greek speakers learning Latin simply by changing the order of the two languages. (By contrast, imagine the number of changes that would be needed to turn a modern textbook for English speakers learning French into one for French speakers learning English.) The bilingualism of the original Colloquia cannot be replicated in this translation, obviously, but because it had some effect on the content it is worth understanding more fully; it is explained in chapter 12, along with other aspects of the history of the Colloquia themselves and the type of language study for which they were designed.

There are six Colloquia; in some passages they are virtually identical, because they were originally all the same text, and in other places they are very different from one another, owing to the way each of the six versions was rewritten independently in antiquity. None is designed to be read as a whole: each is formed of small, separate units suitable for individual lessons. Some of these units have come down to us in excellent condition, but others are fragmentary, and a few make little or no sense in the form in which we have them. What is presented here, therefore, is a set of extracts: only the most coherent version(s) of each unit are given, and the extracts are presented in the order of the original works, that is topic by topic, not version by version.

A good example of the way the different versions overlap is offered by the ancient preface to the Colloquia. This exists in many different versions; some are nearly identical to each other and some almost entirely different. Two of the most different versions are given here to illustrate the range of possibilities.

1.1 THE ANCIENT PREFACE: VERSION 1

Version 1 of the preface (Colloquia Monacensia–Einsidlensia 1a–q and 3a–b) was put together in antiquity from two originally separate texts: the first paragraph of the text below was the preface to a set of bilingual glossaries (for which see chapter 12.2), and the second paragraph was the preface to the Colloquia.

> May this work turn out fortunately! Since I see that many people desire to speak in Latin and in Greek but cannot easily do so on account of the difficulty of the languages and the large amount of vocabulary they involve, I have spared no effort to create a textbook containing all the necessary information. Many other people have tried to do this and failed, since they did not make an effort commensurate with the importance of the matter, but worked for enjoyment or for their own practice; so they have boasted entirely in vain of completing such a book. There is no need for me to say more about them, but I want to make it clear to everyone that no-one has given better or more accurate translations than I have in the three books that I have written, of which this will be the first. In this book I have given a complete

vocabulary in alphabetical order, from the first letter to the last. So now let me begin.

Since I saw that little boys at the beginning of their education need bilingual conversation books so that they can more easily be taught to speak Latin and Greek, I have written briefly below about daily conversation. . . . Conversation practice ought to be given to all boys, both little ones and older ones, since it is essential.

The join between the two originally separate texts is still clearly visible where the writer says he is about to present a complete vocabulary in alphabetical order and then goes on to discuss something completely different; it is notable that over many centuries of copying no-one ever changed this inconsistency.

Both paragraphs make sales pitches by pointing out to the reader the value of the work they introduce; the first of these pitches is especially interesting because it indicates that this work was in competition with other language textbooks. No other trace of these textbooks has survived, and we would not know that they once existed if we did not have this text. It is striking that despite the author's evident pride in his achievement, his name is not attached to the work: we know neither who the 'I' in the passage above was nor, for that matter, the identities of the other people who contributed to the Colloquia. Nor do we know why we do not have their names; perhaps there was a convention in antiquity that authors' names were not attached to elementary works of this type, but it is also possible that a name was originally given and has disappeared at some point in the long process of copying and recopying by which this text was transmitted to us.

The text suggests some uncertainty about the target audience for the Colloquia: one sentence mentions little boys just beginning school, and another mentions older as well as younger children. In fact both older and younger schoolchildren are depicted within the Colloquia as using them.

1.2 THE ANCIENT PREFACE: VERSION 2

The two prefaces that are combined in version 1 are separate in some other versions. Version 2 (Colloquium Celtis 1–2) has only the second preface, the one designed to go with the Colloquia. And this version

FIG. 1 Educated woman with stylus and writing tablets (four leaves, tied together with a ribbon), as depicted on a first-century wall painting from Pompeii, now in the National Archaeological Museum in Naples, Italy (inv. 9084)

has a very different form of the second preface, so different that the historical relationship between the two versions can only just be seen.

> From the 'Elementary Instruction' of Cicero, the chapters concerning daily conversation.
> Practice in everyday conversation ought to be given to all boys and girls, since it is necessary both for little children and for older ones, on account of ancient custom. So let me begin to write, from the beginning of the day to its end.

Perhaps most notable among the differences is the fact that version 2 attributes authorship of the Colloquia to Cicero. The attribution is false; it was probably added in the late antique period by someone who wanted to increase the prestige of this work (of which he was perhaps selling copies) by associating it with a famous Latin author. Such misattributions are fairly common in manuscripts of ancient texts.

This version of the preface makes explicit an important point left unclear in the rest of the Colloquia: the intended users included girls as well as boys. All the children actually depicted in the Colloquia are male, as are nearly all the adult characters – women appear only occasionally, in supporting roles such as wives, mothers, and nurses – so without this statement it would have been reasonable to conclude that girls were not part of the writer's intended audience. Such a conclusion was indeed often drawn before the discovery of this Colloquium, which was published much later than the others (see chapter 12.7). This situation serves to remind us that it is dangerous to draw too many conclusions from silence about women's roles in antiquity: the simple fact that they are not mentioned as participating in a particular activity does not in itself prove that women did not participate.

CHAPTER 2

Days in the Lives of Schoolchildren

Children in antiquity had an experience very different from that found in most modern schools. Rather than being part of a class of people the same age learning the same things, children in antiquity had a largely individual educational experience even when they attended school – something many did not do, as home schooling (whether by parents or by specially hired tutors) was common, and some (perhaps many) children from poorer families were not formally taught at all.

A school often consisted of a single large room (or even an outdoor space), staffed by a main teacher and one or more assistants, containing pupils of a considerable range of ages and levels of attainment. Most pupils were boys, but some girls also attended school, especially at the primary level; likewise, although teachers were normally men, women teachers are occasionally attested. Each child would be given an assignment to do on his/her own and would sit on a bench or chair (or, in some cases, on the ground) and work through it before going up to the teacher to go over it. There were three main types of assignment: reading, writing, and memorisation.

Learning to read is something that most children now accomplish in a relatively short space of time; after that initial period the modern schoolchild is asked to read as a means of acquiring more information, rather than as an end in itself. But in antiquity reading was a skill that took much longer to master and that had to be actively practised for its own sake during much of a child's time in school. The reason is that ancient books were much harder to read than modern ones. Most had no spaces between the words, no distinction between capital and lower-case letters, no paragraph structure, and no punctuation: just a large block of bare letters. Punctuation and word division were not unknown to the ancients, and indeed they were sometimes used in school texts (punctuation is mentioned explicitly in passage 2.3 below, and the diagonal slashes in figure 15 are word dividers), but since they were not normally used students had to learn how to read without

LITTLEREDRIDINGHOODSETOFFONEFINESPRINGMOR
NINGTOBRINGFOODTOHERGRANDMOTHERWHOWA
SILLONTHEWAYSHEUNWISELYSTOPPEDTOTALKTOA
STRANGERABIGBADWOLFTHEWOLFRANTOTHEGRAND
MOTHERSHOUSEATETHEGRANDMOTHERUPANDDRES
SEDHIMSELFINHERCLOTHESWHENREDRIDINGHOODAR
RIVEDTHEWOLFWASINHERGRANDMOTHERSBEDPRE
TENDINGTOBETHEGRANDMOTHERHERSELF

FIG. 2 Modern English prose written with ancient conventions

them. Figure 2 provides an example of what reading with ancient conventions is like when the language of the text is completely familiar to the reader.

The ancient learning-to-read experience was in fact more difficult than figure 2 suggests, because children were often taught to read on archaic poetry rather than on stories written in the kind of language they spoke at home. The most commonly-read work in Greek-speaking schools, from the classical period to the end of antiquity, was Homer's *Iliad*; already in the fifth century BC the *Iliad* must have posed some difficulties for young children, since its language was significantly different from any of the classical dialects, and that problem only increased as time went on. Some sense of the experience of a Greek-speaking child in the Hellenistic period can be gained by attempting to read the *Iliad* in the Dryden translation, which is now more than 300 years old, as illustrated in figure 3.

THEWRATHOFPELEUSSONOMUSERESOUND
WHOSEDIREEFFECTSTHEGRECIANARMYFOUND
ANDMANYAHEROEKINGANDHARDYKNIGHT
WERESENTINEARLYYOUTHTOSHADESOFNIGHT
THEIRLIMBSAPREYTODOGSANDVULTURESMADE
SOWASTHESOVEREIGNWILLOFJOVEOBEYED
FROMTHATILLOMENEDHOURWHENSTRIFEBEGUN
BETWIXTATRIDESGREATANDTHETISGODLIKESON

FIG. 3 Dryden, *Iliad* 1.1–8, written with ancient conventions

WHANTHATAPRILLEWITHHISSHOURESSOOTE
THEDROGHTEOFMARCHHATHPERCEDTOTHEROOTE
ANDBATHEDEVERYVEYNEINSWICHLICOUR
OFWHICHVERTUENGENDREDISTHEFLOUR
WHANZEPHIRUSEEKWITHHISSWEETEBREETH
INSPIREDHATHINEVERYHOLTANDHEETH
THETENDRECROPPESANDTHEYONGESONNE
HATHINTHERAMHISHALFECOURSYRONNE
ANDSMALEFOWELESMAKENMELODYE
THATSLEPENALTHENYGHTWITHOPENYE
SOPRIKETHHEMNATUREINHIRCORAGES
THANNELONGENFOLKTOGOONONPILGRIMAGES

FIG. 4 Chaucer, *Canterbury Tales*, General prologue lines 1–12, written with
ancient conventions

But by the late Roman period reading Homer was much more difficult, closer to what reading Chaucer would be like for us (figure 4).

Latin-speaking children had an easier time, as the classical works of Latin literature were written in the first century B C and first century A D, long after the classical period of Greek literature in the fifth and fourth centuries B C (and, of course, Homer several centuries before that). Ordinary spoken Latin changed over time, just as ordinary spoken Greek did, but during the empire Latin had had fewer centuries to change into something fundamentally different from its classical variety than Greek had had. Nevertheless Virgil, Cicero, and the other classical Latin authors read in schools were not as easy to read as modern children's literature, being full of obscure words and complicated grammar.

Many of the works read by ancient students were tragedies and comedies, in which ancient texts usually lacked speaker designations and stage directions. Ancient readers could normally expect the writer to provide only an indication of which characters were on stage at the start of a scene and horizontal strokes to indicate speaker changes; it was not the writer's job to tell the reader who was speaking or what action was supposed to take place on stage. This convention meant that a tremendous burden of interpretation was placed on the reader in antiquity, as readers had to work out for themselves much information

THREEWITCHES
WHENSHALLWETHREEMEETAGAINE
__INTHUNDERLIGHTNINGORINRAINE
 WHENTHEHURLEYBURLEYSDONE
__WHENTHEBATTAILESLOSTANDWONNE
__THATWILLBEERETHESETOFSUNNE
__WHERETHEPLACE
__UPONTHEHEATH
__THERETOMEETWITHMACBETH
__ICOMEGRAYMALKIN
PADDOCKCALLSANONFAIREISFOULEANDFOULEISFAIRE
HOVERTHROUGHTHEFOGGEANDFILTHIEAYRE

Thunder and lightning. Enter three witches.

First witch: When shall we three meet againe?
                In thunder, lightning, or in raine?
Second witch: When the hurley-burley's done,
                When the battaile's lost, and wonne.
Third witch: That will be ere the set of sunne.
First witch: Where the place?
Second witch: Upon the heath.
Third witch: There to meet with Macbeth.
First witch: I come, Gray-malkin.
All: Paddock calls. Anon! Faire is foule, and foule is faire,
                Hover through the fogge and filthie ayre.   *Exeunt.*

FIG. 5 Shakespeare, *Macbeth*, Act I scene I, written first with ancient conventions and then with modern ones. The spelling and assignment of lines to speakers follow the First Folio.

that is now regularly provided by writers. Consider the different levels of intelligibility of the two versions of the same passage of Shakespeare presented in figure 5, the first of which uses the ancient format and the second the modern one.

In addition to all these problems, ancient texts were all hand-written. Not only was the handwriting sometimes difficult to read, but scribes frequently made mistakes when copying texts, as illustrated in figure 6 (and for the assumption that a copyist would inevitably make mistakes,

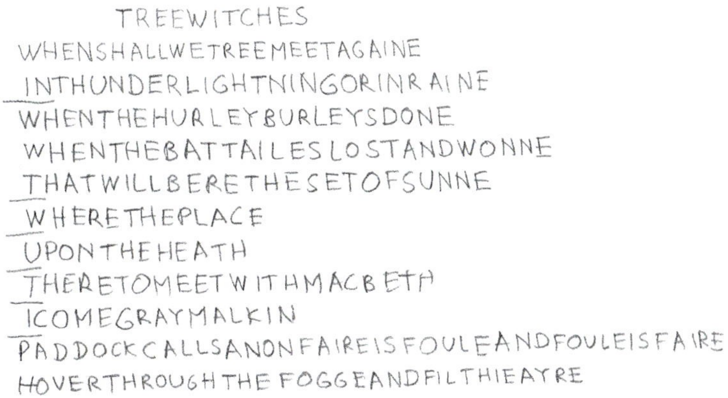

```
TREEWITCHES
WHENSHALLWETREEMEETAGAINE
INTHUNDERLIGHTNINGORINRAINE
WHENTHEHURLEYBURLEYSDONE
WHENTHEBATTAILESLOSTANDWONNE
THATWILLBERETHESETOFSUNNE
WHERETHEPLACE
UPONTHEHEATH
THERETOMEETWITHMACBETH
ICOMEGRAYMALKIN
PADDOCKCALLSANONFAIREISFOULEANDFOULEISFAIRE
HOVERTHROUGHTHEFOGGEANDFILTHIEAYRE
```

FIG. 6 Shakespeare, *Macbeth*, Act I scene 1, inaccurately hand-written with ancient conventions

see Martial's epigram 7.17 in chapter 11.5). A reader therefore had the additional responsibilities of deciphering handwriting and detecting mistakes in the copying. Under these circumstances it is not at all surprising that learning to read fluently was a difficult and lengthy process.

To deal with this difficulty, ancient teachers taught reading in carefully graded steps. Children were not expected to start reading whole sentences as soon as they had learned the alphabet; instead they spent considerable time reading syllables before progressing to words and to sentences. Often children were taught to write before they learned to read, as writing was in some respects considerably easier than reading and as knowing how to write facilitated the process of learning to read. And once pupils did embark on reading continuous texts, they spent a lot of time practising: not only were they frequently asked to read a passage aloud with convincing expression and explain it, but they often prepared these passages in advance, sometimes with the aid of a glossary and/or commentary, and only then performed for the teacher. Pupils reading tragedies and comedies discussed with the teacher the problems of speaker designations; they were not expected to cope on their own until they reached a fairly advanced stage.

For this reason reading aloud before the teacher is the classic school task depicted in the Colloquia: it is often the first task children arriving

FIG. 7 Boy reading from a papyrus roll, as depicted on a first-century wall painting
in the Villa of the Mysteries, Pompeii, Italy

at school are described as doing, and sometimes it is the only thing they
do. Nevertheless other activities also appear. One is writing, which as
already noted sometimes preceded reading. Children are shown writing
their names; this skill is important today but was even more crucial in

antiquity, when a significant number of children never actually learned to read. The ability to sign one's name to a document put one in the category of the literate rather than the illiterate, so it was an important skill to achieve – and far easier than learning how to read the document one was signing. Pupils also copied out verses of poetry, particularly Homer (for Greek speakers) and Virgil (for Latin speakers). This type of activity was individual, like the reading practice: the teacher handed the child a clearly-written model text and expected the child to copy it repeatedly and then to produce the copies for correction.

The third type of assignment commonly depicted in the Colloquia is memorisation and recitation. Ancient children recited from memory not only poetry but also oratorical works, lists of obscure words and their definitions, and grammatical treatises. Knowledge of a large body of vocabulary, including difficult words, was crucial to enable readers to cope with the challenges posed by ancient books: whereas a modern reader can easily identify unfamiliar words in a text and look them up in a dictionary, ancient readers would find it difficult to know where words began and ended unless they already knew the words in question. Thus although dictionaries existed, they were of less use to ancient readers than they are to us, and consequently large-scale memorisation of vocabulary was essential, both in one's own language and in foreign languages.

The goal of memory work at school, however, was not only the acquisition of the material being memorised but also the development of the pupil's memory skills. Many pupils hoped later to progress to training in oratory, and since orators delivered their speeches from memory rather than from a written text or even from notes, they had to have highly developed memory skills. The best speech-writer in the world could not win success as an orator if he could not remember his speeches well enough to deliver them as intended.

In antiquity even highly writing-dependent activities like literary study required a far better memory than they do today, for it was much harder to find something in an ancient book than in a modern one. Until well into the imperial period most ancient books took the form of long rolls (normally about 4 metres in length, but sometimes 10 metres or more), with the writing in many vertical columns (see figure 13). There was often a title at the beginning and/or the end, but very little in the way of tables of contents, indices, chapter headings, line numbers, or other clues to help the reader locate a particular passage. In order to find a specific part of the text one had to unroll the scroll and read through the columns of writing looking for it; the easy skimmability of a modern book (let alone the searchability of electronic texts) did not exist in antiquity. Scholars, therefore, relied heavily on their memories of literary works – though those memories were not always perfect, as many misquotations reveal.

Reading, writing, and memorisation, therefore, were the major tasks in an ancient school. Others also existed: primary-school students often learned basic mathematics, more advanced students wrote their own compositions, and in later centuries (once the everyday spoken

FIG. 8 Woman holding a tablet, as depicted on a second-century marble sarcophagus found near Rome and now in the Louvre Museum in Paris (inv. Ma 495)

varieties of the Greek and Latin languages had become significantly different from the 'correct' written standards) students at all levels learned grammar. Many Latin-speaking schoolchildren also learned Greek, but Greek-speaking children were not normally taught a foreign language at school. That does not mean, however, that people in the Greek-speaking portions of the empire were necessarily mono-lingual: Greek, which had been spread across the areas conquered by Alexander the Great, was the language of (most) education, culture, and government, but in much of the Eastern Roman empire it was not the native language of most inhabitants. Many people in the East grew up speaking a local language such as Coptic or Aramaic in addition to or instead of Greek; some had a fairly limited command of Greek when they arrived at a Greek-speaking school and were effectively educated via a second language.

The writing technologies and physical surroundings of an ancient school were different from those seen today. School exercises were often written on a wax-coated wooden tablet using a stylus (a sharply-pointed tool made of wood, metal, or bone); these could easily be

FIG. 9 Roman wax tablet containing Virgil, *Aeneid* 1.1–7, and stylus (reconstructions)

erased by using the flat back end of the stylus to smooth out the soft wax. Most tablets were small enough to fit comfortably into one hand and therefore did not hold a large amount of text (though ancient children were able to produce surprisingly small writing: at the early stages of learning to write, when modern children may be asked to make their letters 2 cm high or more, ancient children's letters were usually only 1 cm high, and with practice the letter size was soon reduced to 0.5 cm or less; professional scribes frequently produced writing only 0.2 cm high). Tablets could, however, be bound together in groups of two or more to make notebooks that would hold more text (cf. figure 1 above).

Some tablets did not have a wax coating, being either bare wood or wood painted white. To write on these the ancient child used not a stylus but a pen dipped in ink. The wooden tablets were also re-usable, as the ink could be washed off (especially from the white-painted tablets). Both wooden and waxed tablets were commonly used by adults as well as by children; the Vindolanda

FIG. 10 Rosewood pen and pottery inkwell, first or second century, found in Egypt and now in the Louvre Museum in Paris (inv. AF 1372 and E 22599)

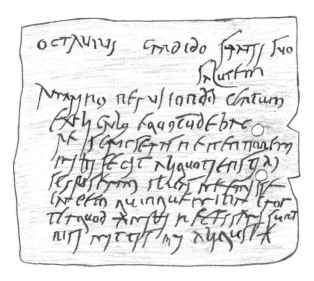

FIG. 11 Vindolanda tablet 343, first page. The writing reads *Octavius Candido fratri suo / salutem. / a Marino nervi pondo centum / explicabo. e quo tu de hac / re scripseras ne mentionem / mihi fecit. aliquotiens tibi / scripseram spicas me emisse / prope m(odios) quinque milia, prop/ter quod d(enarii) mihi necessari sunt. / nisi mittis mi aliquit d(enariorum)* ... A translation of this tablet can be found in chapter 11.3.

tablets from Hadrian's Wall (see figure 11 and chapter 11.3) are good examples.

Children (and adults) also wrote on ostraca, that is, pieces of broken pottery. Ostraca are best known today from the classical Athenian process of ostracism, a political practice in which the citizens wrote on pieces of broken pottery the names of people they wished to banish temporarily from the city. The pottery used for this process was often glazed, and writing was done with a stylus or other sharp implement that could incise letters into the glazed surface. But writing by scratching a hard surface like that of glazed pottery is difficult and inefficient, so it is not suited to writing much more than a single name; when ostraca were used for longer texts the writer normally selected unglazed pottery and wrote on it with a pen dipped in ink. Ostraca were often used in schools, because they were inexpensive, durable, and re-usable (since the ink could be washed off): not only did children practise

FIG. 12 An ostracon from Roman Egypt with the Greek alphabet, first to third century, now in the National and University Library in Strasbourg, France (*O. Stras.* 1.805)

writing on them, but teachers also used them for model texts that could be handled by small children without fear that they might be damaged. Adults also used ostraca for letters and documents; hundreds have been recovered from multiple sites in Roman Egypt.

Paper had not yet been invented, but Egypt produced large quantities of papyrus, a paper-like substance made from the stalks of a reed-like plant. Papyrus was considerably more expensive than paper is today, and unlike most of the other writing surfaces used in schools it was not easy to re-use, so children employed it sparingly. Papyrus sheets are not completely smooth but rather show the fibres of the stalks used to make them; on the front of a sheet these fibres run horizontally, and on the back they run vertically. It was therefore much easier to write on the front, where the fibres provided guide lines for the writing, than on the back, where the vertical fibres got in the way of the pen.

Papyrus was manufactured in sheets, but before being sold the sheets were often glued together to make the long rolls that the ancients used as books. This ancient book form employed only one side of the papyrus, the side that would be on the inside when the book was rolled up. When a book was no longer needed (or no longer

FIG. 13 Papyrus roll containing a passage from the Colloquia (reconstruction based on the fourth- or fifth-century papyrus *P.Prag.* 11.118)

usable – although papyrus is a fairly resilient substance, without the hard covers of a modern book the rolls suffered heavily from wear and tear while being read) it might be re-used for schoolwork. As a result schoolchildren often ended up writing on the back of their papyrus and struggling with the vertical fibres. One common solution to this problem was to cut the used roll into pieces, which could be rotated 90 degrees so that the vertical fibres became horizontal.

In the early imperial period the codex, i.e. a book in the modern format with pages written on both sides and bound together with a spine and covers, made its appearance in Rome (see Martial's epigrams 14.184, 186, and 190, in chapter 11.5). By using both sides of the papyrus, not having a hollow space in the middle of a roll, and often being very large, codices were able to hold far more text than a roll in the same amount of space; the cost of materials was also reduced since half as much papyrus was needed when both sides were used. It took several centuries before the Greek-speaking world fully adopted this innovation, but once

FIG. 14 Man with codex, as depicted on a second-century marble relief from Rome now in the Louvre Museum, Paris (inv. Ma 975)

that had happened the supply of cheap old papyrus for schools largely dried up.

Books could also be made from parchment, that is, leather specially prepared to make a good writing surface. Most parchment was made from sheepskin and therefore came in pieces the size of a sheep; these could be cut and stitched together to make either a codex or a roll. In Egypt parchment was much more expensive than papyrus (though it had the advantage of being re-usable, since it could be treated to produce a surface from which ink could be washed off) and therefore was little used in schools. In some other parts of the Roman empire, where papyrus plants did not grow and where papyrus rolls were therefore relatively expensive imports, parchment may have been more common – though we cannot be sure, since original school documents do not in general survive from these parts of the empire.

The desk had not yet been invented in antiquity; a roll or codex could be rested on a book stand while being read but was often simply held in the reader's hands (see figures 7 and 16). Even when writing, schoolchildren and even professional scribes did not normally have a hard surface on which to rest their writing material. For writing on tablets or ostraca the lack of a desk probably mattered little, since these materials are themselves hard. One could simply hold a tablet in one hand and write on it with the other hand. Papyrus posed greater difficulties, as it is highly flexible; a writer using an ancient pen dipped in ink did not need to press on the papyrus as one does when using modern pencils and ballpoint pens, but nevertheless some kind of backing was needed to keep the papyrus from bending. The traditional solution was for writers to sit down and rest the papyrus either on their thighs or on their tunics, which could be stretched tightly across their legs to provide a relatively firm surface.

Ancient classrooms did not have an equivalent of the blackboard or whiteboard, a surface on which texts large enough for everyone to read could be written and easily erased. The reason for this lack is probably not technological but utilitarian: since each student worked independently and the teacher did not lecture to the class as a whole, whiteboards were not needed. But the walls of a schoolroom might contain material of more long-term utility, the equivalent of our wall posters. A recently-discovered schoolroom in Trimithis, Egypt, has whitewashed walls with poems painted on them in a cheerful red, and poetry might also be written on boards that could be hung up as needed (see figure 15).

Ancient children did not spend all their time on schoolwork; often the afternoons were devoted to physical exercise, and once darkness fell

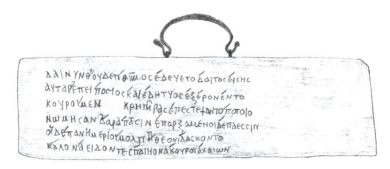

F I G. 15 Wooden board with a passage of Homer designed to be hung on a wall, Roman period, found in Egypt and now in the British Museum, London (inv. GR 1906.10–20.2); partly restored. The passage, *Iliad* 1.468–73, says: 'They feasted, nor was their soul lacking anything of a fitting feast. But when they had overcome the desire for drink and food, youths filled mixing-bowls with wine, and distributed it to all, pouring the first drops in the cups; and the young men of the Achaeans appeased the god with song all day long, singing a beautiful paean.'

it was unusual to do any kind of academic work owing to the expense and poor quality of artificial light. But the writers of the Colloquia were largely uninterested in describing what children did outside school. The scenes involving children often include the early morning, in which children got ready for school, and sometimes describe lunch, which children ate at home (sometimes returning to school afterwards and sometimes not), but they rarely say anything about the rest of a child's day.

2.1 FURTHER READING

For further information on ancient schools and writing see the passages in chapters 11.1, 11.4, and 11.5, books 1 and 2 of Quintilian's *Institutio oratoria* (a particularly good translation, with notes, is provided by Russell 2001); St Augustine's reflections on his schooldays in *Confessions* book 1; Cribiore (2001, a good synthesis of the evidence for Greek-speaking schooling; 1996, a detailed examination of the papyri and ostraca containing school exercises; and 2007, a study of Libanius' rhetoric school in Antioch); Joyal, McDougall, and Yardley (2009, a sourcebook containing a good selection of literary and pictorial evidence); Morgan (1998, a good synthesis of the evidence); Bonner (1977, somewhat out of date but containing much useful information not included in the later works); Bloomer (2015a, a collection of essays of varying quality); Cribiore, Davoli, and Ratzan (2008, presenting the discovery of the classroom at Trimithis); Derda, Markiewicz, and Wipszycka (2007, presenting the discovery of a set of late antique auditoriums in Alexandria; one of these is illustrated below in figure 24); Bagnall (2009, a good introduction to the papyri; note in particular the chapters by A. Bülow-Jacobsen and W. A. Johnson on ancient books and writing materials); and Dickey (2012–15, commentary on the passages quoted below).

2.2 A WELL-OFF CHILD

The child described in this passage (Colloquia Monacensia–Einsidlensia 2a–u) comes from a rich family: he is attended by a nurse, a slave boy to carry his school equipment, and a paedagogue. (The paedagogue was an adult who accompanied children to keep them safe; often he was a slave, but see the papyrus letter *P. Oxy.* vi.930, in chapter 11.4, for a paedagogue who seems to have a rather higher status.) Nevertheless this child dresses himself in the morning, something not to be taken for granted in a culture where even adults frequently relied upon slaves to dress them.

> I woke up at dawn, got out of bed, and sat down. I picked up my leggings and boots and put them on. I asked for water for washing; first I washed my hands, and then my face. I dried myself off. I took off my night-clothes and put on a tunic and a belt; I anointed my head and combed my hair . . . I put on a white hooded cape. I went out of the bedroom with my paedagogue and my nurse to greet my father and mother. I greeted them both and kissed them, and then I left the house.
>
> I went to school, entered, and said, 'Hello, teacher!' And he kissed me and greeted me in return. My slave boy, who carried my case of books, handed me my writing tablets, stylus case, and ruler. I sat down in my place and rubbed out the writing on my wax tablets. I ruled lines following the model. When I had written my exercise, I showed my work to the teacher, who corrected it, crossed

it out, and then ordered me to read aloud. I read until he asked me to pass the book to the next pupil. Then I learned my bilingual textbook thoroughly and recited it.

But right afterwards one of the other pupils gave me dictation practice and said, 'You dictate for me too!'. I said, 'Go do your recitation first!' He said, 'Didn't you see me recite before you did?' I said, 'You're lying! You haven't recited.' He said, 'I'm not lying!' I said, 'If you're telling the truth, I'll dictate for you.'

Meanwhile, as the teacher ordered, the littlest pupils got up to practise the alphabet; they were taught by one of the bigger pupils, who gave them syllables to practise on. Those in the middle group recited in order before the teacher's assistant; they wrote their names or copied verses. And in the top class, I received an exercise to do. We sat down, and I prepared my text using a commentary, glossary, and grammar. When the teacher called me up to read he explained the text to me, both what it meant and who the speakers of the different lines were. Then I answered his questions, such as 'Who is being addressed here?' and 'What part of speech is this word?'. I declined nouns of various genders and parsed a verse.

When we had finished, the teacher sent us home for lunch. I came home, changed my clothes, and received my lunch of white bread, olives, cheese, dried figs, and nuts. I drank chilled water. After eating lunch I went back to school, where I found the teacher reading something over.

The order in which the boy washes and dresses may seem surprising – first he puts on his shoes, then he washes, and then he takes off his night-clothes and puts on his daytime clothes – but it makes good sense in an ancient context. Morning washing involved only the hands and face, since more extensive bathing was done not at home but in the public baths, where one went in the afternoon rather than first thing in the morning. Washing one's hands and face can be done without undressing first, and if the air is cold taking off night-clothes is a step one is inclined to postpone as long as possible. Likewise a cold floor encourages putting on shoes as soon as possible; as the child does not put on trousers, underwear, or any other garments that need to go over the feet, having his shoes on already is no impediment to his later getting dressed. (Although we have no independent evidence for the shape of ancient night-clothes, this passage suggests that they were shaped like a modern nightgown, not like pyjamas; otherwise they would probably have been removed before the shoes were put on.)

The child does not eat breakfast before leaving for school; Romans did not normally eat breakfast, and this fact is reflected in the Colloquia, which never mention breakfast. The only two meals of the day are lunch (for which children returned home from school) and dinner.

Upon arriving at school the boy greets the teacher, a ritual followed by every schoolchild in the Colloquia. Schools did not have a fixed start time – children simply got to work when they arrived – so some other pupils were probably already present when this boy arrived, and one was probably working with the teacher. Having the teacher stop what he was doing and greet each pupil as he or she arrived must have been fairly disruptive, but it was clearly an accepted feature of ancient schools.

The boy then goes through all three of the main school occupations: reading, writing, and memorisation. The work memorised is a bilingual textbook (perhaps even this Colloquium?); the child is

FIG. 16 A student arriving at school greets the teacher, as depicted on a second-century sandstone relief from a tomb at Neumagen, now in the Rheinisches Landesmuseum in Trier, Germany (inv. Nm. 180a 2); partly restored. Note the boys reading from rolls (the roll on the left is on a wooden case or book-rest) and the absence of desks

therefore learning a foreign language and so must be a Latin speaker in the Western empire.

Two children have a squabble, apparently without intervention from the teacher. Ancient classrooms were fairly noisy, what with the sound of children performing their readings and recitations in front of the teacher(s) and other children practising their own readings or recitations, and this noise would have made it harder for a teacher to hear children talking to each other. It is also likely that the teacher was not constantly looking at the class, as he would have had to concentrate on the individual currently performing in front of him. Nevertheless teachers tried to keep the pupils under control as best they could (cf. Philogelos joke 61 in chapter 11.1).

In this classroom the pupils are divided into three groups. The youngest ones are at the syllable stage of learning to read (i.e. they have learned the alphabet but not yet progressed to whole words); they are taught by one of the older pupils, who writes out syllables for them to practise reading – or perhaps dictates syllables for them to write down to practise writing. The middle group, working with the teacher's assistant, has reached the stage of writing words and verses, while those in the top group, to which the narrator belongs, work with the teacher himself and try to decipher longer passages. The narrator prepares his passage with a commentary, glossary, and grammar; these aids suggest that the passage is in a foreign language but do not absolutely prove it, since a difficult piece of poetry in the child's native language could also have required such resources.

The narrator's passage is probably from a tragedy or comedy, as part of the reader's task is working out who the speakers are; the teacher first explains who is speaking and then asks the child to say who the words are addressed to, in order to test his overall comprehension of the scene. The child's grammatical knowledge is tested in multiple ways: by identifying the parts of speech of words in the passage, by listing the various different forms that the nouns used in the passage could appear in ('declining' nouns), and by giving a complete grammatical explanation of a verse (e.g. what the subject and object are, the names of the forms in which each word occurs, and the reasons for the particular constructions used; this is known as 'parsing' a sentence or verse).

2.3 A MODEL CHILD

Roman education made heavy use of examples of good and bad behaviour; the idea was that a child who saw good actions praised and bad ones censured would grow up to imitate the good rather than the bad. Often the virtues and vices concentrated on were ones peculiar to adults: the brave soldier who risked his life to save the state versus the coward who shirked battle and faced opprobrium, the wise and honest statesman who led the people successfully through difficulty and could not be bribed versus the criminal or thug, etc. But in this story of a perfect schoolboy (Colloquium Stephani 1–39) the virtues in question are ones suited to children: the boy is perfectly clean, neat, and well behaved as well as being an excellent student.

Read well!

What did you do today?

When I was woken up in the morning, I called my slave boy. I told him to open the shutters, and he did so quickly. I got up and sat on the frame of the bed, asking him to bring my shoes and leggings, for it was cold. Once I had my shoes on he gave me a clean towel and a little jug of water to wash my face. I poured it first over my hands and then washed my face, remembering to close my mouth, and I scrubbed my teeth and gums, remembering to spit rather than swallow. I blew my nose, and when I was completely clean I dried my hands, arms, and face. It is important for a free-born boy to be clean when he goes to school.

Then I asked someone to bring my book and stylus, and handed them to my slave boy to carry to school for me. When I was all ready I went forth in auspicious fashion, with my paedagogue following me. I went straight through the colonnade that led to the school. Whenever I ran into people I knew, I greeted them, and they greeted me in return. When I came to the staircase, I went up it one step at a time, without running, as a boy should. Arriving in the school vestibule, I took off my cloak and hung it up, and I smoothed down my hair.

Then I lifted the curtain over the doorway and entered the school. First I greeted the teachers and my fellow students, as a polite child should. Then I wrote my name, and waited while those ahead of me recited, paying attention to their pronunciations and especially to that of the teacher. This is how we learn: from paying attention when something is being explained to others. In this way one both progresses and achieves self-confidence.

Then I sat down in my usual seat, extended my right hand and drew back the left one, and recited my lesson, just as I had received it to learn. I recited poetry in metre, with proper pauses for full stops and for commas, and with the sound *h* pronounced where it should be. I also gave a paraphrase of the poetry. While I was reciting the teacher corrected my mistakes, so that I would develop a better speaking style.

I came forward, handed over the tablet containing my lesson, and produced from memory an outline of the things I had done. Then, when the teacher dismissed me, I settled down in my seat. I took my language textbook and copied out conversational phrases. I asked the teacher questions, and once they had been answered I read my work aloud to the teacher, who explained the text carefully to me, until I understood who speaks which lines and what the poet's words meant. Then I read at sight, quickly, a little-known work that I had never seen before.

Everyone did such things, one by one, but with different assignments depending on the ability and level of advancement of each individual, as well as how much time they had available and how old they were. The teacher also took into account the pupils' different characters, because there are some who have a difficult attitude to hard work. And literary study is hard work, for even when you make good progress, more still remains to be done before you reach the peak of achievement.

So some were just reciting lists of nouns, and others recited poetry, according to the levels they had attained in their literacy studies. They got up and stood by the words painted on the wall. Some of the beginners were taught by one of the more advanced students, who gave them basic information and taught them how to count using their fingers and counting-stones. While they did these things, I recited to the teacher. Other pupils had free time for explanations and for asking questions, in two classes, a slower group and a faster group.

A Grammar Lesson

There are five cases of nouns: nominative, genitive, dative, accusative, vocative, and ablative. Nouns all have number: singular for one, dual for two, and plural for three or more. What verb is this? How many persons are there? 'You say' is second person, and 'he says' is third person . . .

A Lesson on the Trojan War

May he be a worthy descendant of the ancients we read about in Homer, the great kings who led the Greeks and who were wise, both young and old. They considered an injury to one of their citizens to be an injury to them all, so they unanimously determined that they would either punish Paris or die in the attempt. (Paris had sailed with a fleet from Troy to Greece and had been entertained as a guest by king Menelaus of Sparta, but he thought nothing of Menelaus' kindness to him, his hospitality, or indeed even basic human decency, for he acted like an unthinking barbarian and snatched away Menelaus' wife Helen and took her to the land of Troy, where his father Priam was king.) So they quickly gathered a great army and collected many ships to contain the multitudes of men they had assembled from many places both on the mainland and on the islands. The supreme command went to king Agamemnon, but there were also many other leaders, whose prowess we admire and whose wisdom we praise. These all sailed to Troy, where they accomplished many memorable deeds as they fought for nine years against the Trojans; and in the tenth year they destroyed the city. All the important Trojans were killed except Aeneas, who escaped to become the founder of the Roman state, and in this way the Greeks took Helen back. But as a result many men who were outstanding for their courage and noble birth died, either in the war itself or from storms on their way home afterward – or from despair.

Other Lessons

While we were practising these things, the time for dictation practice arrived. So I took up my writing tablets and wrote from the teacher's dictation an extract from a speech of Demosthenes, not a whole speech but as much as the time allowed. I put in the punctuation marks correctly. I watched the others recite, and then I recited myself.

The instruction 'Read well!' at the start of the Colloquium seems to be addressed to children using this Colloquium as a reading exercise. They are addressed only here, and the story is then framed as the child's answer to the question 'What did you do today?'.

The first thing this child does in the morning is to get his slave to open the shutters, in order to get some light into the room so that he

FIG. 17 Window with partially surviving shutters at the Villa of the Mysteries (Pompeii, Italy), first century; originally there would also have been a third shutter leaf on the right

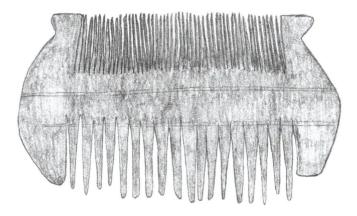

FIG. 18 Roman-period wooden comb found at Oxyrhynchus, Egypt, and now in
the British Museum, London (inv. GR 1911.6–6.4)

can see to get dressed. Then, like the child in the previous passage, he
puts on his shoes and leggings and then washes – but the rest of the
dressing scene is omitted altogether, leaving us with the interesting
impression that this child goes to school in his nightgown (or, if he did
not wear anything at night, naked apart from the shoes and leggings).
The writer may have got so carried away describing the model child's
faultless cleanliness that he forgot to mention clothing, but it is also
possible that the story has been damaged in transmission and
a description of getting dressed has been lost.

This child owns a book that he brings to school; this marks him
both as an advanced pupil (since in the initial stages of education
students did not use books) and as someone rich enough to own this
fairly expensive item. His family's wealth is, of course, also apparent
from the child's slave boy and paedagogue.

On the way to school the child displays perfect Roman politeness in
greeting all the acquaintances he meets; his good behaviour is also
demonstrated by going sedately up the stairs, one at a time. Upon
arrival at school he makes an effort to make sure he is looking neat and
tidy before entering the classroom.

This child greets on arrival not only the teachers but also the other
pupils already present, all of whom then stop what they are doing to
greet him in return. It is notable that despite his perfection the narrator

is not the first child to arrive at the school: perhaps the teacher who wrote this text wanted to stress the importance of greeting the other pupils on arrival, something the first pupil to arrive could not do.

Because one of the other pupils is working with the teacher when the narrator arrives, the narrator has to wait to be given his first assignment of the day. No doubt newly-arrived pupils in this position had a tendency to get bored and cause trouble, but this one not only waits patiently but also does what most teachers can only dream of in their pupils: he learns from the instruction aimed at others as well as from that aimed at him personally.

When it is his own turn to recite, the narrator of course does a perfect job: not only has he memorised the words of his passage, but he has also mastered the finer points of its delivery. He expresses the rhythm, the punctuation (it is not clear whether this is punctuation that the boy knows should be there or punctuation actually written in the text), and the sound *h* (which had largely disappeared from ordinary conversational language in both Greek and Latin by the middle of the empire). In order to demonstrate his complete under-standing of the poem, the boy also expresses its content in his own words ('paraphrase').

The passage has become slightly confused about the location of the child. Initially he seems to be reciting from his seat, with the teacher standing near him, but this arrangement was unusual in antiquity: typically the child studied in his seat and then in order to recite went and stood before the teacher, who normally remained seated in a chair at the front of the class. Moreover, after reciting the child comes up to the teacher, who now seems to be in his traditional location, and hands over his tablet as if he is to begin again from the start. Probably the order of this scene has been somewhat disrupted in transmission: most likely the boy originally stood before the teacher to recite, then sat down and studied, and then came up again with his tablet.

This child is clearly a Latin speaker, for he is using a language textbook, portions of which he writes out in order to acquire his own copy. It was common for more advanced schoolchildren to make their own copies of the texts they would read; not only was this much cheaper for the parents than paying someone else to copy out the book, but it meant that by the time the child started using the book he had some awareness of its contents (not necessarily a full awareness, given the extent to which reading was more difficult than writing in antiquity, but enough to give him a head start in reading it).

The narrator then works on a tragedy or comedy, with its difficulties of speaker attribution, before reading aloud a text he has not prepared. This last was an exceptionally difficult skill and marked out a particularly good student; it is especially impressive that this boy can read the unknown text quickly.

Up to this point the story is clearly aimed at schoolchildren: the virtues described are ones adults want children to have, and the virtues of the teacher are not emphasised. But the ancient writer, who would himself have been a schoolteacher, here inserts a passage about the virtues of a well-run school; this moralising must be directed not at children but at other teachers. It is interesting not only because it shows us what the writer thought the ideal form of teaching was, but also because it indicates that the writer expected other teachers to use his work: he was consciously writing for publication, not just producing material for his own students to use.

The ideal of teaching, according to this writer, is meeting each student's individual needs. A teacher should give each pupil a different task, varying not only according to the children's ages and abilities and how advanced they are, but also according to their characters. Literary study, the writer admits frankly, is hard work, and even when a student has achieved a considerable amount he or she will still have a long way to go before mastering the subject; some pupils have a better relationship with hard work than do others, and this needs to be taken into account when setting their assignments.

In the grammar lesson that follows the language being studied was originally Greek; one can tell this from the inclusion of the dual number (used in Greek to refer to two people or things, as the singular is used for one and the plural for three or more). Admittedly Roman-period spoken Greek did not have a dual any more than Latin did, but a dual was needed in order to read Homer and Plato and was therefore learned in schools. Also pointing in the direction of Greek is the statement that there are five cases (forms into which nouns and pronouns can be put to indicate their grammatical function: 'he' and 'him' are in English two different cases of the same word), since Latin has six cases. The actual list of cases, however, contains six, including the ablative, a case found in Latin and not in Greek: evidently a later user of this text did not realise that the list of cases was supposed to apply to Greek rather than Latin and added the case he thought was missing.

The next lesson is a summary of the Trojan war (from a Roman perspective, since it emphasises the role of Aeneas). This is expressed as a story told by the teacher to the pupils; it was probably something they had to read aloud, copy out, or memorise. The passage has a very different style from the rest of the Colloquium, with long sentences containing nesting parenthetical clauses (in the original, in fact, a single gigantic sentence takes up most of the passage); it would have been extremely difficult to understand in the ancient format and would therefore have been a task suited to a particularly advanced student.

Finally the narrator undertakes a dictation exercise, from a speech of Demosthenes (another difficult text with very long sentences). The writer hastens to emphasise that the dictation does not involve a complete speech, for Demosthenes' speeches are famously long; the passage chosen is suitable to the time available. The narrator is, of course, as good at dictation as at the other types of school exercise: he is able to add correct punctuation to reflect the meaning of the words he hears.

2.4 A STUDENT IN THE GREEK EAST?

Unlike the children in the two previous Colloquia, the child in these dialogues (Colloquium Harleianum 3a–10g) is depicted as learning Latin. One might conclude on that basis that he is a Greek-speaking child in the Eastern empire, except that such children did not learn Latin at school. Probably this dialogue was originally composed in the West about a child learning Greek and then adapted for use in the East, i.e. teaching Latin to Greek-speaking adults or law students. It is difficult to tell how much the adaptor has changed: the main character is still clearly a child, a feature that has to come from the West, so the changes have not been severe – but some details of the educational environment might come from an Eastern law school rather than a Western primary school.

A New Pupil

PUPIL (*to slave boy*): Get up, boy; why are you lazing around? Pick up all the Latin books, the parchment notebook, the tablets, the casket, the ruler, the ink, and the pens. Let's go, let's greet the teacher. (*to teacher*) Hello, sir teacher! May all be well for you. From today I want to work hard, so please teach me to speak Latin.

TEACHER: I shall teach you, provided that you pay attention to me.

PUPIL: Look, I'm paying attention!

TEACHER: You speak well, in keeping with your good birth. In that case, pass me the book-stand and the book, turn to the right place in the book, and read with your mouth properly open. . . . Now mark the place well, so that you can write an exercise.

Paying Tuition

TEACHER: Have you got the tuition money with you? Why not?

PUPIL: I asked my father for it, and he said, 'I'll bring it myself, soon, so that I can see a sample of your progress at the same time.'

TEACHER: In that case you need to study hard so that you'll be prepared when he comes.

PUPIL: I'm already prepared, because I lit a lamp and studied after dark yesterday.

TEACHER: You have done well; I'm pleased with you!

Problems with Writing Equipment

TEACHER: Put another coat of white paint on your tablet, sit down, and write. Why are you just standing there – don't you understand what I just said? Put long vowel marks on your letters. Add a little water to your ink; see, now it flows better.

PUPIL: Pass me the pen and the penknife.

TEACHER: Which knife do you want?

PUPIL: I want the sharp one.

TEACHER: Why do you want that one?

An Accusation of Truancy

TEACHER: Yesterday you played truant, and at midday you were not at home. I went to look for you and heard everything you did from your nurse.

PUPIL: The person who spoke to you is lying: my father took me with him to the praetorium. The magistrates greeted him personally, and he received letters from the emperors. When he got them he immediately went up to the temple and offered sacrifice for the eternal preservation and victory of the emperors. Only after that did we come down. He's an important judge, you know: today he started hearing cases at dawn.

TEACHER: You can always think of an excuse, can't you? You don't seem to realise that time off from school results in an ignorant boy. Now show me your writing. Do you call that good? You really deserve to be flogged, but I'll let you off this time. For now, go and have lunch, and come back reasonably quickly afterwards. Have a good time!

PUPIL: May all be well for you.

This Colloquium probably consists of a set of separate dialogues, with no assumption that the same child and teacher participates in them all. The short dialogues were suitable for reading or memorisation as separate lessons. In the first one we see a student who is evidently new at the school, or newly returned after a lapse in attendance, for he has to convince the teacher to take him on as a pupil. He does this not by promising payment (though payment is required, as both parties know), but by promising hard work and agreeing to pay attention. The teacher's psychologically astute request for the attention is complemented by his lavish praise of the student once agreement is reached.

In the second dialogue a student arrives without the tuition fees due to the teacher; these were paid at the end of each period of teaching, not at the beginning as in modern fee-paying systems, so the teacher could not simply tell the child that he was not entitled to attend school until the tuition was paid. The child explains that his father intends to bring the money in person later that day. School started very early in the morning, so the father's timing may indicate that he did not want to get up as early as his son did – but the father may also have had other commitments early in the morning, for example the early-morning greetings that traditionally took place between patrons and clients (see Martial epigram 4.8 in chapter 11.5; for another case of a father not coming with the tuition money, see the papyrus letter *SB* 111.6262 in chapter 11.4).

The father has asked for a demonstration of his son's progress before the tuition money is paid. This type of request was common in antiquity, in part because teachers, like other professionals, had no formal qualifications. Anyone could set himself up as a teacher (or as a doctor, veterinarian, etc.), and there was no obvious way of verifying whether such people had the knowledge they claimed to have; many jokes circulated about poor-quality teachers (see Philogelos jokes 61, 140, 197, and 220 in chapter 11.1). A responsible father therefore kept a close eye on his children's education, making sure that they had actually learned something before paying the teacher for the teaching. Unfortunately for the teachers, this system left impecunious parents with considerable latitude when they wanted to evade paying fees: all a father had to do was claim that his children had not made sufficient progress, and he could legitimately refuse to pay for their education. The teacher was then faced with a choice of expelling the children from his school, thereby guaranteeing that he would never get his money, or continuing to teach them in hopes that the father would eventually decide to pay up.

Understandably, therefore, the teacher becomes nervous at the child's statement that his father wants a demonstration of his progress; he exhorts the boy to prepare carefully for that demonstration. But the boy, an exemplary character, reassures the teacher that he is already fully prepared, having done homework after dark the previous evening (or before dawn earlier that morning). Such lamplit study was the mark of a particularly diligent student, both because the oil needed to keep lamps burning was expensive and because lamps did not give much light. Ancient books were hard enough to read in daylight; reading by lamplight was exceptionally difficult. The teacher is therefore effusive in his praise of the boy.

The next dialogue concerns the materials used for writing and the problems that could arise with them. Painted wooden tablets needed to

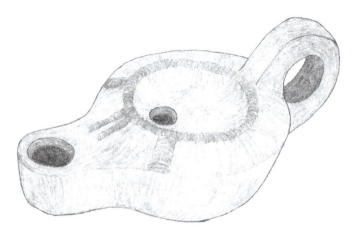

FIG. 19 A Roman-period pottery lamp from Colchester (British Museum, London); the hole on the left is where the wick emerges and burns, and the hole in the middle is for adding more oil

be periodically repainted; sometimes this task was done at home, but here the pupil is instructed to do it in school. Ink was placed in open inkwells for ease of use (see figure 10 above), and many inkwells were made of porous unglazed pottery, so the water in the ink gradually evaporated, making the remaining ink thicker and harder to use. Pupils had to learn when their problems with writing were caused by overly thick ink and discover how much water to add in order to give the ink a good consistency – if it was too thin and watery the writing produced would be faint and hard to read. And since ancient pens were made of soft substances such as reeds rather than of metal, their fine nibs quickly wore down and became blunt; this was particularly a problem when writing on ostraca, which were often rough and abrasive. Pens had to be recut frequently, so schoolchildren needed to learn how to recognise the signs of a worn-down nib and how to recut it.

The last dialogue opens with a serious accusation, truancy. Major delinquency was regularly punished by whipping in ancient schools, so the ancient reader for whom this work was written probably antici-pated, as he read it, that it would contain a description of a whipping. Interestingly, however, there are no descriptions of whipping in the

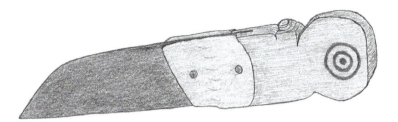

FIG. 20 Roman pen knife with iron blade and wooden handle, first to third century
(Xanten Archaeological Park, Germany)

Colloquia: it was evidently a feature of ancient education that teachers preferred not to dwell on. Instead the boy has an excellent excuse: his father, an important local official who this morning is judging court cases, took him to town yesterday on important business involving letters from the emperor (for fathers taking their children on business trips see *P.Oxy.* 1.119 in chapter 11.4). Although rhetoric teachers and other instructors at advanced levels might have a high status, teachers of children normally had a low social standing, so by making this point the child is implicitly pulling rank on the teacher. The excuse is entirely successful; the teacher, though grumpy, is unable to administer any punishment whatsoever. Ancient children must have greatly enjoyed reading about this child's triumph over his teacher. The writer of this dialogue, no doubt a low-status teacher himself, displayed considerable psychological acuity in thus encouraging his students to enjoy their work.

2.5 WINNING A SCHOOL COMPETITION

These short dialogues (Colloquium Montepessulanum 2a–g, 6a–b) come from a Colloquium that, having been extensively rewritten in the East, has largely lost its school scenes. The first shows a new student promising enthusiasm and attention in order to learn Latin, and the second depicts the winner of a school version of the Capitoline games. This contest, undertaken not by the young pupils seen in the earlier Colloquia but by more advanced students who had reached the stage of being able to compose, memorise, and perform their own speeches before an audience, involved speeches in praise ('panegyrics') of Capitoline Jupiter.

PUPIL: Hello, teacher! I want, I very much desire, to learn to speak Greek and Latin, so please teach me, teacher.

TEACHER: I'll do that, if you pay attention to me.

PUPIL: I am paying careful attention to you.

TEACHER: So, since you really want to learn the Latin speech, I shall show you, son, that it cannot be mastered by just anyone: knowledge of Latin is the attainment of those who are both well-educated and naturally intelligent. For that reason I am happy to teach you. You will need to pay attention to my recommendations, for an expert speaker is created from a combination of listening, memory, understanding, and daily practice. . . . And, of course, I shall need some money from you.

*****

PUPIL: I have written a panegyric.

TEACHER: Of whom?

PUPIL: Of Capitoline Jupiter.

TEACHER: Read it to me. (*after hearing it*) You have spoken magnificently. Take the crown; no-one can compete with you.

2.6 AN ABBREVIATED VERSION

This Colloquium has been abbreviated, so that almost all its scenes are stripped to their essentials. Nevertheless it has a few features not seen in the other Colloquia, including a realistic squabble between children over who has taken whose seat and a complaint about unsuitable wax on a tablet. (Wax, though soft and malleable when warm, becomes hard and brittle in the cold, so children going to school in the winter must often have found it difficult to use their tablets effectively.) Like the child in the first Colloquium, this boy goes home for lunch and then returns to school; he does not stay for the whole afternoon, however, but has time for a trip to the baths. The original version of this passage (Colloquium Leidense–Stephani 1a–9b) contains many alternative phrases for extra vocabulary and grammar practice, but these have been omitted here.

The sun has risen; it is already light. He got up from the bed; he was up late yesterday. 'Dress me! Give me my shoes and socks and trousers. Now I have my shoes on. Bring water to wash my hands. My hands are dirty.' Now I have washed my hands and face; I dry them and go out of the bedroom.

I go to school. First I greet the teacher, who greets me in return. 'Hello, teacher! Hello, fellow pupils!' 'Fellow pupils, give me my place! Move over!' 'Go over there; this is my place; I got it first.' I sit down and learn; now I understand my lesson. Now I am able to recite my lesson. 'Translate this for me, write!' I was given an assignment and did it; then I began to read verses.

A boy said, 'I don't know how to rule lines on my tablet. You do it for me, since you know.' 'I can't do it either; the wax is too hard. It ought to be soft.'

I asked the teacher to let me go home for lunch, and he dismissed me. I said goodbye to him, and he said goodbye in return. After I had eaten I returned to school and recited again. I said to my slave boy, 'Give me a tablet!' And the others as well recited their work, with pauses in the right places. I went through my reading, because it was nearly time to go to the baths.

Then I went off and ordered my slaves to carry the towels, and I followed the others who were already on their way to the baths, greeting them one by one and saying 'May it be well for you!', 'Have a good bath!', and 'Have a good dinner!'

2.7 AN EXPANDED VERSION

This Colloquium, in contrast to the preceding one, has been expanded. The expansion was evidently effected by taking two or three different Colloquia, cutting them up into scenes, and joining the pieces together so that all the material for one type of scene ended up together, followed by all the material for another type of scene. (The process is in fact fundamentally the same as the one I have used to arrange extracts from the Colloquia in this book, except that the ancient expander did not add explanations between the different extracts.) The result is that the child repeats the same activities over and over again: first he asks his nurse to dress him, then he dresses himself, then he dresses himself again, then he asks for yet more clothes and washes, then he leaves the house, only to return home shortly afterwards in order to say good morning to his family before leaving again for school. Like the previous passage, this one (Colloquium Celtis 3a–45c) includes much extra vocabulary that has been omitted here.

'Nurse, dress me and put on my shoes! It's time for us to go to school early, before the break of day.' In the morning, when I first woke up (and I woke up early), I got out of bed and first took off my night-clothes and put on a linen shirt, underwear, a mantle, leggings, a tunic, and my other clothes. Then I woke up my slave boy and said to him, 'Get up, boy, and see if it's light yet; open the door and the shutters.' And he did. Then I said to him, 'Give me my things, pass me my shoes, fold up and put away the clothes I am not wearing. Give me underwear and a mantle.' 'Here they are.' Then I got off the bed, put on my belt and mantle, and dressed as is appropriate for the son of a respectable family. I asked for shoes, trousers, socks, and leggings. I was given water to wash my face, and I washed. I rinsed out my mouth and dried myself with a clean towel. 'Bring clean water to my brother too, so that he can go to school with us.' Then I ordered the slaves to bring us a tunic, a shirt, and a white hooded cloak.

When we were ready, we prayed to all the gods and asked them for good fortune for the whole day. Then I went out, with the slave boy who carried my books. Whenever I ran into a friend or acquaintance, I greeted him by name, and he greeted me by my name in return: 'Hello, sir! May all be well for you!' Then I returned to my father's house. I went to greet my parents and the rest of my family. I went off again to school.

I entered the school and said, 'Hello, teacher!', and the teacher greeted me in return. He handed me the book-stand and ordered me to read five columns of writing to him, and I read accurately and fluently. Then I passed the book-stand to another student and went to the teacher's assistant. I greeted him and the other students, and they greeted me in return. I sat down in my regular place on the bench, and when I was seated the boy who carried my books passed me my writing tablets, case of styluses, ruler, counting board, and counters. First I erased the writing on the tablets and ruled lines following the model, and then I wrote. I showed my writing to the teacher, and he praised me because I had written well. I read aloud what I had written, with pauses in the right places. I recited. Another child said, 'I recited before you did.' 'You're lying!' 'I'm not lying!' Then my paedagogue said to me, 'It's time to leave, so that we can go to your Greek teacher and your Latin teacher.' The teacher dismissed us to these other studies.

I entered the school of the Greek teacher and that of the Latin teacher. I learn my assigned work thoroughly: if I am already prepared when I come to school, I recite at once, but if not, I read my work again first. I read aloud in front of the class. I was given an assignment to do. An unfamiliar work was explained to me. I was given a passage, and along with some other students I read it immediately; others read the same passage after preparing it carefully.

The little children practise in front of the teacher's assistant: language textbooks and syllables, the inflection of the verb, the whole grammar book, conversation, the cases of nouns, the genders of nouns, their numbers, compositional status, and inflections, words in alphabetical order, letters, vowels, and consonants. They pronounce their readings with the right pauses and intonations. Then they go through lists of nouns classified by subject, and the eight parts of speech.

Then there is silence. The more advanced students go up to the teacher; they read a text about the *Iliad* and another about the *Odyssey*. They are assigned a passage, a rhetorical exercise, a history, a comedy, stories, an explanation of the causes of the Trojan war, the basis for a recitation, the speeches of Cicero, Virgil, Persius, Lucan, Statius, Terence, Sallust, Theocritus, Thucydides, Demosthenes, Hippocrates, Xenophon, and the Cynics. Then they all go back to their seats, and each one does the work assigned to him: one writes and another learns a speech. When they have done their work they recite in order, each according to his ability. If someone has recited well, he is praised; if badly, he is punished. We are dismissed around the seventh hour.

When the instructor orders, the littlest children stand up to read syllables, and we older ones recite an exercise and verses for the teacher's assistant. They recite vocabulary words and Colloquia; they write a lesson. The second class reads aloud. I am in the first class, and we sit down. I go through my commentary, glossary, and grammar until I am called up. Finally the teacher dismisses us, giving us a holiday for tomorrow. Everyone goes home.

I enter my father's house, take off my good clothes, and change into my ordinary clothes. I ask for water to wash my hands. Since I am hungry, I say to my slave boy, 'Set out the table and put the tablecloth on it, and a napkin, and go to my mother to get bread and relish and a drink of wine for me. Tell her that I have to go back to school in the afternoon, and for this reason bring lunch quickly.' I have had enough to eat and drink, and the table is taken away. I get up to work on my writing practice.

When he finally arrives at school this boy seems to stay a relatively short time before moving on to a second school, where he stays until lunchtime (the seventh hour: for Roman time reckoning see the explanation of passage 3.3). He then moves on to a third school and only after that returns home for lunch, which he has to eat quickly in order to return for yet more school. There could be more reality to this process than appears at first sight, since ancient children often attended more than one school. Different teachers taught different things: music, mathematics, shorthand, and rhetoric, for example, might all be taught in different schools from the 'grammarian's' school that focussed on reading, writing, and the study of literature, so the more advanced pupils in the 'grammarian's' school frequently attended one or more other schools as well. Nevertheless it is not clear that the three school scenes given here represent three different schools, since all three contain little children at the syllable stage of literacy acquisition (though in some other ways the middle scene looks as though it could come from a more advanced school) and because of the chronological problems of fitting all three into the morning. Probably different versions of a scene in a grammarian's school have simply been strung together.

Unsurprisingly this Colloquium repeats many of the features found in the others, but a few are new. This child's clothing includes underwear, a type of garment sparsely attested for antiquity but known to have existed (see figure 21). The family has morning prayer; this is clearly not

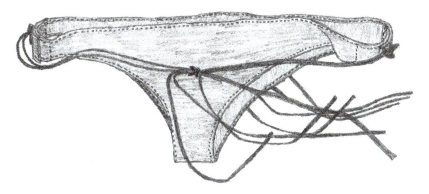

FIG. 21 Roman leather underpants, reconstructed on the basis of a garment found in London (Xanten Archaeological Park, Germany)

FIG. 22 Miniature bronze altar for home devotions, second or third century, found in Egypt and now in the Louvre Museum in Paris (inv. E 11901)

a Christian addition, as they pray to 'all the gods'. The presence of this obviously pagan reference shows that this text cannot have been significantly rewritten after Christianity took over the education system, as it is exactly the sort of thing that a Christian teacher would want to remove from a book designed for children.

This child's school equipment includes a counting board and counters. The counting board was a device somewhat like an abacus that was used for mathematical calculations. One common format for a counting board using Roman numerals is shown in figure 23, which illustrates how subtraction was done with such a device. The methods we use for subtraction with Arabic numerals are not suitable for Roman numerals, which have no zero and use M for 1,000, D for 500, C for 100, L for 50, X for 10, V for 5, and I for 1.

In this Colloquium the youngest children, who in other Colloquia are taught by one of the older pupils, work with the assistant teacher. They work on syllables, as in the other Colloquia, as well as on bilingual language textbooks (thus indicating that they are in the West) and on grammar. The amount of grammar being learned by

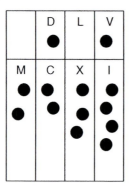 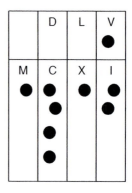

FIG. 23 One common layout of Roman counting boards. The squares in the upper row have space for only one counter each, as Roman numerals never use these letters more than once in a single number; the squares in the lower row have space for up to four counters each, as these letters can be used up to four times in a single number. (In some versions of Roman numerals subtraction is used to prevent letters being used more than three times in a single number, e.g. IV rather than IIII for 4. This system is not used with counting boards: 4 is IIII, 40 is XXXX, etc.) The board on the left shows the number MMDCCXXXVIIII (2739), while that on the right shows the result of subtracting MCCCXXII (1322) from the board on the left.

these young children seems to be significant; that may indicate that they are learning a foreign language, or it could indicate that the setting is in the later empire, when native speakers of both Greek and Latin had to learn grammar in order to write their own languages well.

The more advanced pupils are reading about the Trojan war, but not from Homer or Virgil; rather they are reading simplified summaries of the literary classics, perhaps like the one in passage 2.3 or perhaps longer ones. Such summaries survive in large numbers; although to our eyes they lack most of the appeal of the *Iliad* and *Odyssey*, since they reduce the great epics to prose plot summaries, they had the considerable advantages of being both much more comprehensible and much shorter than the original poems. Similar summaries existed for the classical Greek tragedies; sometimes these summaries survive when the plays themselves do not, allowing us to know the plots of lost tragedies and indicating that some ancient scholars found the summaries more worth copying than the plays themselves.

The list of authors given in this passage is surprising, as it does not fit well with other evidence on which texts were used in school. The comedian Menander, a staple of the school curriculum to judge from the papyrus survivals, seems to be absent, while the doctor Hippocrates (poorly represented in papyri and a writer whose works are inherently unlikely to have been used in educational establishments other than medical schools) is included.

CHAPTER 3

Let's Go to Court

The second half of the Colloquia describes the day of an adult. For the most part the scenes are arranged in the order in which activities would actually take place on a typical day: court cases, other business, lunch, bathing, dinner, and bedtime. There are variations between the different Colloquia, however, and in one the court scene occurs in an epilogue tacked on to the end.

One of the main reasons why Greek speakers learned Latin was to become lawyers. In theory, Roman law required all legal business to be conducted in Latin, and fluency in Latin was therefore essential for entry to the profession. The reality was more complicated: in Greek-speaking areas much legal work was in fact done primarily or exclusively in Greek, but Latin remained useful. The major works of Roman law were all in Latin until the sixth century, so before then a Latinless lawyer would have been unable to consult them. Moreover, for most of antiquity certain legal documents, including the wills of Roman citizens, had to be written in Latin in order to be valid; of course most citizens in Greek-speaking areas wanted to compose their wills in Greek, but they would hire a lawyer to make the official Latin version, and therefore lawyers were better off if they could write enough Latin to produce these documents.

In the East, therefore, one of the main places the Colloquia were used and adapted was law schools. Entry into law school was not as difficult as it is today: there were no strict limits on the number of students, no standardised exams to pass in order to gain entry, and no major outlays of money at the start (for an outsider's opinion of the intelligence of ancient law students, see Philogelos joke 54 in chapter II.I). As a result many students began to study law without a serious commitment and later dropped out; others switched from one law school to another, since there were no particular obstacles to doing so. The income and prestige of these schools depended on the number of students they could attract and retain, sometimes in the face of fierce competition.

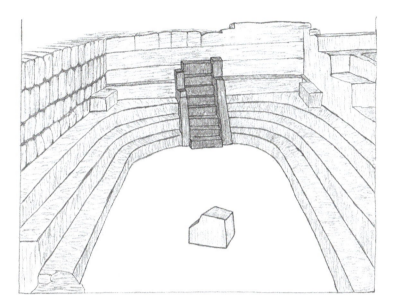

FIG. 24 Auditorium of a late antique law school (Kom el-Dikka auditorium K at Alexandria, Egypt): the teacher sat at the top of the steps at the back, the student whose turn it was to declaim stood at the podium in the centre, and the other students sat on the stone seats around the sides to watch and evaluate the performance

As a result of this situation, the teachers who used, adapted, and expanded the Colloquia in the East needed to encourage their students to continue studying. One result of this concern was the introduction of legal materials into the language-learning curriculum. Eastern Latin teachers produced a bilingual treatise on the Roman law of manumission (the freeing of slaves), so that elementary Latin students could begin with material directly relevant to their studies – though as the Latin of this treatise is very difficult, it was perhaps not the most successful method. Probably more useful was a bilingual set of stories about the legal judgments of the emperor Hadrian (the Roman empire's equivalent of King Solomon in terms of legal wisdom); these stories were shorter and considerably easier than the manumission treatise, but they must still have been challenging for beginners.

The Colloquia were considerably easier than both these legal texts and therefore more widely used, and teachers in the law schools made them more attractive to law students by adding short lawcourt scenes. These descriptions of court cases all tend to emphasise how easy the life of a lawyer will be for those who finish their legal training. Lawyers in the Colloquia always win their cases and are well rewarded by grateful clients, but they are never shown exerting any particular effort to achieve this effect. A lawyer who becomes unemployed will quickly be offered a job, simply because he deserves one after all that study.

This rosy picture of the lawyer's life was almost certainly unrealistic: not only must there have been a losing side as well as a winning side to every court case, but without any controls on the numbers entering the profession, there were no doubt many fully-trained and highly deserving lawyers who nevertheless did not find work. Often the relationships between lawyers and their clients were less than perfect (see Martial, epigrams 6.19 and 8.17 in chapter 11.5), and the court system did not always have a good reputation (see Philogelos joke 264 in chapter 11.1). The scenes below, therefore, were an overly optimistic effort at encouraging students to stick with their legal studies; as such they represent an early version of a type of mis-selling of education that, needless to say, would never be practised today . . .

3.1 FURTHER READING

For further information see the second-century Roman legal textbook by Gaius (e.g. in Gordon and Seckel 1988, which provides the Latin text and a translation) and the sixth-century *Institutes* of Justinian (e.g. in Birks and McLeod 1987, which offers a translation and excellent introduction), Cribiore (2007, on Libanius' Greek school of rhetoric, which competed with Roman law schools and with other Greek establishments), and Dickey (2012–15, commentary on the passages quoted below).

3.2 WINNING A LAWSUIT

This passage (Colloquia Monacensia–Einsidlensia 4a–p) is the longest and most detailed of the court scenes. It begins with a chance encounter between two friends, Gaius and Lucius. (These are *praenomina* or first names and would not actually have been used in conversation by real Romans of the imperial period; the names are employed here to make the scene generic and to give it a Roman flavour.)

The master of the house went out and met his friend and said, 'Hello, Gaius!', and he kissed him. And Gaius greeted him in return, saying, 'I hope you're well, Lucius; it's been ages since I saw you!'

LUCIUS: How are you doing?

GAIUS: Everything's going well. How are you?

LUCIUS: I'm glad to hear it! But as for me, I have a court case.

GAIUS: In which court? The quaestor's?

LUCIUS: No, not there.

GAIUS: So where? The proconsul's court?

LUCIUS: No, the magistrates' court, where it was transferred by the governor's response to a petition.

GAIUS: What sort of case is it?

LUCIUS: Not a big one; it's a financial matter, you see. Actually, if you have time, I'd like you to join us. The judges have given us today as a court date, when the verdict will be declared, so I want to have you there when I consider the case with my lawyers.

GAIUS: So you have hired lawyers?

LUCIUS: Yes.

GAIUS: Which ones?

LUCIUS: Your friends.

GAIUS: Well done! Have you got a meeting fixed? When and where?

LUCIUS: In the forum, in the portico, near the stoa of Victory.

GAIUS: I have to do something first, but I'll be there soon.

LUCIUS: Please don't forget!

GAIUS: Don't worry; I will take care of it. (*departs*)

LUCIUS (*to his slaves*): Let's go to the bank and get a hundred denarii to give the lawyers so that they will defend us better.

SLAVE: Here is the banker.

LUCIUS: Get the money from him and follow me. (*arriving at the forum*) Good, Gaius is here as we agreed; let's call him into our discussion. Gaius, here we have the evidence.

GAIUS: Did you serve him a summons?

LUCIUS: Yes.

GAIUS: Did you produce evidence?

LUCIUS: Yes.

GAIUS: Get ready, then.

LUCIUS: I am ready.

GAIUS: Your opponent is trying to interrupt.

LUCIUS (*to the opponent*): Be quiet!

OPPONENT: I am not making any noise!

LUCIUS: Keep silent, everyone: let's listen to the verdict. (*after the verdict*) Gaius, did you hear? We've won!

The initial discussion gives the writer an opportunity to run through the different courts in which a case could be heard, as well as useful greeting vocabulary. Then, after agreeing to come to Lucius' conference with his legal team, Gaius goes off on other business, while Lucius goes to the bank to get money to pay that legal team. (How well they are paid is not completely clear, unfortunately, as the passage is hard to date: the Roman empire suffered from severe inflation, so although a hundred denarii represented a very considerable sum in the early empire it would not have been impressive in the late empire. See chapter 11.8.)

The legal conference, involving only discussion that would have looked easy even to a student at the very beginning of his legal studies, seems to merge imperceptibly into the court hearing itself, for the opponent (who would not have attended a conference between Gaius and his legal team) is clearly present by the end. His efforts to speak, however, are easily put down, meaning that the legal team does not have the difficult task of responding to any actual arguments. Perhaps unsurprisingly in these circumstances, the judge decides in favour of Gaius.

3.3 TWO CRIMINAL TRIALS IN THE FORUM

People outside the legal profession often think of lawyers primarily in connection with criminal trials, but criminal cases make up a comparatively small percentage of all legal work, dwarfed by wills, property transactions, lawsuits, etc. The same was true in antiquity, and this reality is reflected in the legal scenes of the Colloquia, which only once mention criminal trials. That one mention, however, is intriguing.

This passage (Colloquium Celtis 70a–77c) begins, unusually, by re-introducing the child who was the central character of the first part of the Colloquium; the narrator (probably his paedagogue) encourages him to engage in the ultimate virtuous activity of the schoolboy, study by lamplight (cf. passage 2.4 above). The narrator then moves on to describe early morning in the forum of a provincial city. (That the setting is a provincial capital is suggested by the presence of the governor, who would be less likely to appear either in Rome or in a lesser provincial city; it is, however, possible that the governor is envisioned as visiting the city.) At least five important officials are described as working in the forum at this hour, engaged (for the most part) in government tasks that such officials would actually have undertaken. (For the exact nature of the tasks and the occasional difficulties in reconciling them with other evidence, see Dickey 2012–15: 11.251–8.)

About Working at Night and Business in the Forum . . .

Get up, child, get up quickly and study even though it is night, so that you will have a good outcome. To the best of my knowledge this is the way for you to excel at your recitation tomorrow. (*later*) Now you can rest a little, while my master, your father, goes to the forum at daybreak. He is going early because the prefect, provincial governor, treasury official, military chief, and estate manager have all gone out to the forum. You can even hear the voice of the herald as he summons the leading citizens and the ordinary people.

Each official in the forum is doing his allocated task. The prefect is attending to the requisition of military clothing, the provincial governor is dealing with the horses that need to be approved for use by the army, the treasury official is inspecting the gold and silver recently collected, the military chief is approving the new recruits to the army, the treasury official is collecting the income from the licence-fee of animal fodder and of barley, the estate manager is receiving the yields of wheat and spelt, and the centurions are collecting the copper tax revenues.

At the third hour the lawyers enter: advocates, pleaders, legal advisers, and those heading to the private courts. They will conduct very many cases, as many as each is able to carry out given his literacy skills. There are also cases that have reached their time limits, and I think those will have to be finished today.

Then the governor comes to the speaker's platform to take his seat. The platform is all arranged, and the judge arrives at it. Through the herald, he orders the people on trial to be hauled to their feet. A guilty robber is made to stand up and is interrogated as he deserves: he is tortured, racked, hung up, stretched, whipped, beaten with cudgels – all the tortures in order. But still he denies that he is guilty. He must be punished, so he is led off to execution.

Then another accused person is made to stand up, an innocent one. He has a large legal team, with learned men supporting him. And indeed he is successful and is acquitted. The witnesses too come off well in his case, for they are released without being tortured. This case has a lavish defence, and each person involved signs the record to certify its truth.

The courts open at the third hour of the day, that is, around nine a.m. Romans divided the day into twelve hours of equal length, beginning at sunrise and ending at sunset, and the night was made up of another twelve hours. (In the summer, therefore, the hours of the day were longer than those of the night, and in the winter vice versa, but the sixth hour of the day was always at our noon and the sixth hour of the night at our midnight.) For other evidence that the courts opened at the third hour see Martial, epigram 4.8 (in chapter 11.5).

The narrator describes a panorama of the arriving legal profession before focussing on two trials. The first is of a robber; he has no lawyer attending him and (for that reason?) is manifestly guilty. Annoyingly, however, he refuses to confess despite an impressive string of tortures. The list of tortures, unfortunately, is likely to be realistic: although at an early period Roman citizens were exempt from judicial torture, that exemption was gradually eroded during the empire until most people could be tortured.

In the Roman legal system the proper result of such non-confession should have been that the defendant, if judged guilty, had the right to appeal, but in this case he is simply executed. The writer does not suggest that anything might be wrong with this outcome, probably because he sees the defendant as being guilty and considers execution the correct outcome when the defendant is in fact guilty.

The second trial is very different; this defendant is attended by a lavishly-funded team of learned legal advisors and is (for that reason?) completely innocent. In fact he is so innocent that the writer does not bother to mention what he was accused of. Perhaps he is tortured a bit, but if so there is no mention of that fact; the witnesses in his case are expressly stated not to have been tortured, which must have been a relief to them as torture of witnesses was common during the empire. The defendant is released without a stain on his reputation, a fact that the writer implicitly connects with the good legal defence.

3.4 THE EASY LIFE OF A LAWYER

The writer of this scene (Colloquium Harleianum 12a–f) suggests to students whose enthusiasm for their studies may be flagging that if they can only manage to complete the course, they need never fear unemployment. An unemployed lawyer is depicted as encountering a rich man who, hearing that he is available, immediately entrusts him with the management of a court case. The reasons for his choice are not that the rich man urgently needs a lawyer, nor that he knows this lawyer to be particularly good or skilled in the particular area of law the case concerns, but rather that the unemployed man deserves to be employed.

The use of 'dearest' as an address between men who are clearly not very close seems odd today but is unsurprising in the Roman empire, when a wide variety of apparently affectionate terms were regularly deployed between friends and even distant acquaintances (cf. 'brother' and 'sister' in the Vindolanda tablets, chapter 11.3). The affection often seems to be expressed by the less powerful member of the pair to the more powerful one, as here.

UNEMPLOYED LAWYER: Hello, sir! I hope you will be well forever, dearest. How are your affairs? Is everything going well?

RICH ACQUAINTANCE: It is going as the gods desire. And how are you doing?

UNEMPLOYED LAWYER: Until just recently I had jobs, but now I do not have one.

RICH ACQUAINTANCE: In that case, let me entrust you with running my court case. Let's go; walk along with me, and I'll tell you what to do. You must have a job, for you are worthy of all good things.

3.5 ANOTHER WAY TO RESOLVE A DISPUTE

Dispute resolution did not have to involve recourse to the courts. Turning to the gods for help might be faster, cheaper, and equally effective, as this passage (Colloquium Leidense–Stephani 10a–e) suggests.

> He said to me, 'Take an oath to what you have just said, unless you are perjured.' And I swore most truly, and did not perjure myself: 'By the best and greatest god, and by my wish that that god be kind to me, and by the health of anyone you can think of, I shall not be found perjured in this oath.' Then he believed me.

The gods were widely believed to pay close attention to oaths sworn in their names and to punish anyone who dared invoke them when swearing falsely. (Thus the Second Commandment, 'Thou shalt not take the name of the Lord thy God in vain', originally meant not that one should not say 'damn', but that the Jewish god, like the Greek and Roman ones, would punish anyone who attached his name to a lie.)

This belief operated in two different ways to prevent people from swearing falsely in the name of a god. Many people simply believed that the god would punish them if they lied and were therefore unwilling to do so (for a parody of the consequences of this belief, see Philogelos joke 226, in chapter 11.1). Some others were more sceptical and would have been willing to take the chance, but even for them there was an obstacle to swearing falsely. Because of the important social role that belief in the gods filled in the ancient world, atheists were a problem for society, for they could not be relied upon to operate under the same constraints as other people. An atheist would not necessarily ever tell the truth; moreover he might draw the wrath of the gods down on the entire population by committing sacrilege. So ancient societies tended not to leave punishment of atheists to the gods, but rather to take matters into their own hands. Anyone who was enough of an atheist to swear falsely in the name of a god and was proved to have done so could expect repercussions from his fellow-citizens even if the god did not bother to act.

Even today, the court system relies on a two-pronged approach to getting people to tell the truth: those giving evidence are asked to swear on the Bible to tell the truth, and if they are later shown to have lied under oath, they can be punished by the courts for doing so. Perjury (lying under oath) is a serious crime, despite the fact that under most other circumstances our penal code does not consider lying to be criminal.

In antiquity, the severity of an instance of false swearing depended on the extent to which the god was directly involved. To be really convincing, an oath had to be taken in a way that the god concerned would be sure to notice, such as in his or her temple. The god also had to be specifically named; the lack of a name here is because this is a generic scene, adaptable for an oath by any god. And to make an oath convincing the swearer had to put on the line something that mattered to him, such as his life, his health, or the health of his family. Here the swearer invokes both his own future prosperity and the health of anyone his opponent cares to name; this is a convincing oath.

CHAPTER 4

Financial Transactions

Financial transactions are today, and were in antiquity, something learners of a foreign language are concerned to get right, for mistakes in this area can cause more trouble than most other kinds of errors. The Western writers of the Colloquia were not very concerned with this fact: their audience of children was learning Greek as the language of literature and culture rather than for practical purposes. The Eastern writers, on the other hand, faced an audience with practical needs and tried to cater to those needs – and not all their audience consisted of future lawyers. A number of banking and shopping scenes were therefore added in the East.

The Roman world had a well-developed banking system, but the banks lacked formal regulation and controls. In addition to established banks, individuals could, and often did, make loans to one another. These loans could cause several kinds of problem: a lender might find it difficult to get the borrower to repay the loan, and a 'borrower' might be pursued for money not actually owed. The Colloquia include one scene of borrowing money, one of returning money, and two of unsuccessful attempts to get money returned; this ratio may not be far distant from reality.

The Colloquia also include several shopping scenes; an expedition to buy clothing is given here, and food shopping is depicted in passage 7.2.

4.1 FURTHER READING

For further information see Jones (2006, an engaging study of a small group of bankers and their work), von Reden (2010 and 2012, overviews of Roman finance), Holleran (2012, on shopping), Harris (2006, on the role that credit and other forms of money other than coins played in the Roman economy), Andreau (1999, an important study of Roman banking), and Dickey (2012–15, commentary on the passages quoted below).

FIG. 25 Financial transaction as depicted on a second- or third-century tomb relief from Neumagen, now in the Rheinisches Landesmuseum in Trier, Germany (inv. Nm. 303); partly restored. Note the seal ring on the man at the right, the bound tablets on the left, and the men counting and inspecting the coins piled on the table

4.2 A TRIP TO THE BANK

In this passage (Colloquia Monacensia–Einsidlensia 5a–6a) a polite and encouraging banker is depicted as happy to lend a large sum without collateral. This situation may not be unrealistic, as bankers no doubt chose their tactics depending on their knowledge of the borrower and the likelihood of eventual repayment. In this case the banker's confidence is fully justified, for in the following scene the borrower repays the money.

BANKER: What would you like, sir?

BORROWER: Do you have any money to lend?

BANKER: What do you need to borrow?

BORROWER: If you have it, lend me five thousand sesterces.

BANKER: Certainly – even if I had not had it in stock, I would have rustled it up from somewhere for you.

BORROWER: Do you need collateral?

BANKER: Heavens, no! I'm sure we will not need that. Just write for me a statement that you borrowed the money.

BORROWER: What interest rate should I put down?

BANKER: Whatever rate you want.

BORROWER: I have written the statement.

BANKER: Thank you; now put your seal on it.
BORROWER: Done.
BANKER: Now count the money.
BORROWER: Done.
BANKER: Check it over and make sure there are no bad coins.
BORROWER: Done.
BANKER: Be sure to return the money in good coins, just as you
    received it.
BORROWER: I promise to satisfy you when returning it.

Later, when the borrower comes to repay the loan:
BANKER: You have come on an auspicious day!
BORROWER: Yes, I have!
BANKER: Did you come up with the repayment money?
BORROWER: Yes, I did.
BANKER: Have you given it to the clerk?
BORROWER: Yes, I have.
BANKER: Then you are discharged from your debt.
BORROWER: Do you need anything else from me?
BANKER: Only that you fare well in the future!

A notable feature of this passage is that interest is charged on the loan, and the interest rate is specified in the loan contract. Nominally the borrower and lender were free to agree on any interest rate they choose, up to the legal maximum of 12%, but in practice there was often a standard rate known to both parties (this varied by time and place but was often either 6% or 12%). Thus in this passage the borrower politely offers to pay the rate suggested by the banker, and the banker politely leaves it up to the borrower to specify the rate, but probably neither offer is to be taken at face value.

The borrower filled in the contract and ratified it not with his signature but with his seal; this was a carved stone, usually worn on a ring, that would be pressed into a blob of melted wax dripped onto the document to make a relief image. Each man of substance had his own distinctive seal, which would often be immediately recognised by his associates. In case of doubt the seal impression on a document could be compared to the ring worn by the alleged participant in the deal; if they matched, any attempts at denial were usually futile.

FIG. 26 Roman seal ring with distinctive design (Romano-Germanic Museum, Cologne, Germany)

After signing the contract the borrower is asked to count the money, to make sure that both sides agree on the amount actually handed over before the money leaves the bank. The borrower is then asked to check for substandard coins, something that was a serious problem during the empire: a coin that was not made from the metal it was supposed to be made of (debased), or that had been trimmed to remove some metal out of which other coins could be made (clipped), was worth less than its face value. The request to check for bad coins protects the banker as much as the borrower: having declared before leaving the bank that all the coins he received were sound, the borrower would be in a very weak position to return later with a bad one and claim that he had received it from the banker. As an additional precaution, the borrower expressly promises not to include any bad coins in the money used to repay the loan.

A repayment scene immediately follows the borrowing scene, but the writer was probably not trying to suggest that loans were repaid as soon as they were taken out; rather the two transactions are grouped together since they use related terminology.

FIG. 27 A clipped coin compared to a similar coin in its original condition (fourth-century *siliquae* from the Hoxne Hoard, now in the British Museum, London)

4.3 TWO ATTEMPTS TO RECOVER LOANS

In each of these passages (Colloquium Montepessulanum 19c–d and Colloquium Harleianum 23a–i) Gaius tries unsuccessfully to recover money lent to Lucius. In the first passage Lucius frankly admits to owing the money but is unable to hand it over on the spot. In the second he denies ever having borrowed it, maintaining that he is the victim of mistaken identity. This type of denial could have been countered by producing witnesses to the original loan or a contract with Lucius' seal on it, and Gaius could have attempted to enforce his claim in a court of law. But none of these routes are taken, a fact that may indicate that Gaius' claim is not very strong.

Instead Lucius offers to take an oath that he is not the real debtor, in any temple Gaius chooses (for the significance of this offer see passage 3.5 above). Gaius accepts the offer and, when Lucius goes through with the oath, accepts that he was wrong about the identity of the borrower.

> GAIUS: How wonderful to run into you like this! I was looking for you in the forum earlier today – I'm talking to you, sir! Could I have back the money that you owe me?

LUCIUS: I'll give it to you tomorrow.

GAIUS: You're playing with me.

LUCIUS: I am not!

*****

GAIUS (*to himself*): Hey, isn't that man Lucius, the one I lent money to? Yes, it is; I'll go over and greet him. (*aloud*) Hello, sir. Could I now have back my money, which you've owed me for ages?

'LUCIUS': What on earth are you saying, you insane person?

GAIUS: I lent you money, and now you call me insane? Swindler, don't you recognise me?

'LUCIUS': Get out of here and look for the person you really lent it to, because I never borrowed a penny from you.

GAIUS: Can you swear to that for me?

'LUCIUS': I'm happy to swear anywhere you want.

GAIUS: Let's go to the temple, then: swear for me there, if you dare!

Later, in the temple:

'LUCIUS': By the god of this temple, I swear that you never lent me any money.

GAIUS: Very well; I accept your oath. Respectable free men should not quarrel.

4.4 A SHOPPING TRIP

Ancient shopping was not like going to a store today. Often prices were not fixed in advance but were negotiated by bargaining between buyer and seller. Shoppers could be accompanied by a retinue of servants; the most important function of the servants was to carry the goods purchased (cf. passage 7.2, where perishable food is sent home immediately after purchase in the care of one servant while others continue with their master to buy more food), but they might also do the bargaining and hand over payments. (It is often assumed that only slaves performed menial services in the Roman empire; but there really is no evidence that freedmen never filled this type of role for poorer patrons. I use the word 'servant' as a general term for people who perform menial services,

FIG. 28 A *paenula* as depicted on a first-century terracotta figurine from Ruvo, Italy, now in the British Museum, London (inv. GR 1856.12–26.236)

whether free or slaves.) This passage (Colloquium Montepessulanum 13b–f) has been damaged; some material is missing in the middle.

> GAIUS: I'm going to the clothes merchant. (*once there*) How much is that?
>
> SELLER: A hundred denarii.
>
> GAIUS: How much is the cape?
>
> SELLER: Two hundred denarii.
>
> GAIUS: You're asking a lot; I'll give you one hundred denarii.
>
> SELLER: I can't sell it for that! That's what I pay the wholesalers for a cape . . .
>
> GAIUS (*to servant*): Let's go to the linen-merchant; you do the bargaining with him.
>
> SERVANT: Give us underwear and four linen towels. How much for them all?
>
> SELLER: Three hundred denarii.

A particularly interesting feature of this passage is the specific prices for clearly identifiable garments. Of course, the price initially suggested by the seller is likely to be artificially high and that initially suggested by the buyer artificially low, because of the bargaining process, but in the case of the cape (*paenula*, a long hooded garment) both prices are given, allowing us to calculate the likely value of the garment as a hundred and fifty denarii. This price is one-thirtieth of 4,500 denarii, the average of the prices for a cape in the year 301, when Diocletian attempted to stem the empire's rampant inflation by publishing an edict listing the maximum allowable prices for all sorts of goods and services (see chapter 11.8). Information on the inflation rate in the centuries leading up to that Edict can allow us to calculate the approximate dates at which items listed in the Edict would have had other prices, leading to a date of the early second century for capes priced at one hundred and fifty denarii. This passage is therefore likely to have been composed around that date.

CHAPTER 5

Supporting Friends

Friendship, for the Romans, entailed not only enjoyable companion-ship but also obligations. A Roman was expected to visit his friends when they were ill and to show up in court to support them when they needed it, as well as keeping in regular touch.

5.1 FURTHER READING

For further information on Roman friendship see Cicero's treatise *De Amicitia* ('On Friendship'), Williams (2012, a look at literary and non-literary texts bearing on the subject), Fitzgerald (1997, a collection of essays on friendship in different ancient sources), Konstan (1997, a study of friendship in Greece and Rome), and Dickey (2012–15, commentary on the passages quoted below).

5.2 VISITING THE SICK

In this passage (Colloquia Monacensia–Einsidlensia 6b–j) two of Lucius' friends, having heard that he is ill, resolve to visit him; this was a common social duty in Rome (see Philogelos jokes 34 and 70 in chapter 11.1).

> FRIEND 1: Why don't you come with us?
> FRIEND 2: Where are you going?
> FRIEND 1: To visit our friend Lucius.
> FRIEND 2: What is wrong with him?
> FRIEND 1: He's ill.
> FRIEND 2: Since when?
> FRIEND 1: He fell ill a few days ago.
> FRIEND 2: Where does he live?
> FRIEND 1: Not far away; please come there with me. (*later*) I think this is his building. Yes, it is. There is the doorman; ask him if we may come in to see his master.

FIG. 29 Reconstruction of part of a Roman *insula*, based on a drawing by Italo Gismondi reconstructing the House of the Thermopolium at Ostia (Calza 1923: 58). The large shuttered openings on the ground floor are shops (note the small windows directly above them, which light the mezzanine lofts), and the much grander windows and balconies above them belong to the expensive housing on the middle floor; note the progressively smaller windows of the upper floors. In reality, the only time such a building could have appeared this unpopulated is the middle of the night.

DOORMAN: Who are you looking for?

FRIEND 1: Your master: we have come about his health.

DOORMAN: Go on up.

FRIEND 1: How many flights of stairs?

DOORMAN: Two. When you get to the landing, knock on the door on the right – that is, if he has come back. He went out.

FRIEND 1 (*after going upstairs*): Let's knock.

SERVANT (*opening the door*): Who is it? Hello, everyone!

FRIEND 1: We want to pay a visit to your master. If he is awake, tell him that I am here.

SERVANT: He is not here.

FRIEND 1: What are you saying? Where is he?

SERVANT: He went down to the laurel grove to take a walk.

FRIEND 1: We congratulate him! When he comes back, tell him that we came to see him and were delighted to hear about his complete recovery.

SERVANT: I shall do that.

Lucius lives on one of the upper floors of an *insula* or multi-storey block of flats (cf. Philogelos jokes 193 and 194 in chapter 11.1), so visiting him involves not only going to his building but then negotiating with the doorman for permission to enter the building. The doorman tells the friends which flat Lucius is in and how to get to it, and they proceed up the stairs to the flat indicated. When they knock on that door it is opened by Lucius' servant, who informs the visitors that his master has recovered and gone for a walk. Lucius seems to be moderately well off, for he lives up only two flights of stairs: many Roman *insulae* had shops on the ground floor (often with mezzanine lofts in which the shopkeeper's family lived), large dwellings for the rich on the floor above, and then progressively smaller and poorer dwellings with each successive flight of stairs.

5.3 RESPONDING TO AN APPEAL

Lucius is in a state of undress, perhaps still in bed in the morning, when a messenger arrives from his friend Gaius, bearing a letter asking for Lucius' immediate assistance with important business. Showing himself an exemplary friend, Lucius hastens to get ready to come to his friend's assistance (Colloquium Montepessulanum 4a–g).

SERVANT: Who is knocking on the door?

MESSENGER: A messenger from Gaius to Lucius. If he is here, tell him that I have come.

SERVANT (*to Lucius*): Someone is here from Gaius.

LUCIUS: Ask him in. (*to messenger*) What is it, boy? Is everything all right?

MESSENGER: Yes, sir. He has sent you a sealed letter.

LUCIUS: Give it to me, let me read it. (*after reading the letter*) He has asked me to come and help him with important business. Go, boy, and tell him that I am on my way. (*to slaves*) Give me my shoes! Bring water to wash my face! Give me my tunic and put on my belt. Drape the toga on me, and give me the rings. Why are you just standing there, friend? Gather up the things we need and come with me! I am on my way to help an old friend, a senator of the Roman people, one who traces his ancestry from Romulus and from Trojan Aeneas.

The business for which Lucius' help is needed is probably in the Senate or the courts, for he asks the servant to drape a toga over his tunic (it was common for members of the higher social classes to be dressed by their servants). The toga was a formal garment largely reserved for legal and government business, in part because it was so impractical that no manual labour could be performed in it. Its role is nicely illustrated in Livy's version of the Cincinnatus story: an official delegation arriving at Cincinnatus' farm to tell him that the senate had asked him to assume supreme power over Rome in a military emergency found him working in the fields and therefore wearing only a tunic. Instead of telling him at once that there was an emergency, they asked him to put on his toga and only then communicated the news (Livy 3.26.9–10).

The formal dress involved here also includes rings, which were important as they included the identifying seals that Lucius could use to ratify a document (cf. passage 4.2 and figure 26).

The friend is identified as an important person in emphatically Western terms: he is a senator and one of the original noblemen descended from Romulus and Aeneas. The Western setting is provided for the same reason that modern French textbooks normally provide texts with a French setting and German textbooks provide texts with a German setting: a foreign language and its culture need to be taught together. Although in principle all the adult scenes in the Colloquia seem to have this Western setting (the characters' names are always clearly Roman rather than Greek, on the rare occasions that places are named they are always in the West, and cultural features are generally Western), it is rare for the Romanness of the setting to be emphasised quite as much as it is in this passage.

FIG. 30 Second-century statue of a Roman man wearing a toga (Romano-Germanic Museum, Cologne, Germany, inv. 2009.25)

5.4 MAKING PLANS

Friendship was, of course, a source of enjoyment as well as obligation. In this passage (Colloquium Harleianum 21a–22c) friends plan a dinner for four tonight and a trip to the gladiatorial show and the baths tomorrow; they might have included another friend as well (the man is referred to as 'my brother', but that term could be used for friends and acquaintances in the Roman world), but he is hiding out of shame arising from having engaged in a drunken brawl the previous day.

FRIEND 1: Let's go out to bathe together.

FRIEND 2: Where shall we bathe?

FRIEND 1: Wherever you want!

FRIEND 2: Because today is a feast day, for our meal tonight they have got us vegetables, good salt fish, fresh fish, cooked foods, meat, sweet wine, and chickens.

FRIEND 1: That's great!

FRIEND 2: There are four of us for the meal.

FRIEND 1: And where will our feast be?

FRIEND 2: Wherever you want; let's make it a shared enterprise.

FRIEND 1: But let's be sure to have some simple people with us, because it's much more refreshing to relax with such people.

FRIEND 2: My brother has sent his excuses. Yesterday he had a brawl at the baths, which he was forced into by some friends who were drunk, and now he is too embarrassed to appear in public.

FRIEND 1: If all goes well, the day after tomorrow there will be a circus and gladiatorial games. Let's watch them together and then go to the baths with him when the games finish.

FRIEND 2: Whatever you want to do is fine with me!

5.5 REBUKES FOR NEGLECT

Friendships could, of course, run into trouble, and sometimes Romans needed to rebuke their friends for neglect. In the first of these passages (Colloquium Harleianum 13a–b) a man is accused of ignoring a friend on the previous day, and in the second (Colloquium

Harleianum 26a–d) and third (Colloquium Harleianum 27a–e) friends (the term 'brother' is not to be taken literally) are rebuked for neglect. In the generic formula given in the second passage a whole set of alternatives for describing the neglect are provided so that the language learner can pick the one appropriate to his particular situation. The provision of such material suggests that the need for rebukes of this type may have been felt relatively often.

> FRIEND 1: The day before yesterday I greeted you up in the temple, and you didn't pay any attention to me.
> FRIEND 2: I was absorbed in praying.
> FRIEND 1: It looked to me as though you were absorbed in the friend you were talking to.

*****

What is it, brother – why didn't you come to the temple / home / to the forum / to the lecture hall / to the judge / to the ex-consul / to town / to our country estate / to our brother? I waited for you, and on account of you I had to eat my lunch late!

*****

(*To messenger*) Go to my brother and say to him, 'What have we done to you to make you neglect us? I am fond of you; in fact I love you, by the god / by heaven / by the sun / by the earth / by my own survival. And you yourself know that you are our friend.'

CHAPTER 6

What to Say when Things do not go so Well

Although most portions of the Colloquia contain coherent narratives or dialogues, some consist of collections of phrases, like a modern phrasebook. These phrasebook sections are probably the original format for the Eastern half of the Colloquia; most of them were gradually turned into coherent vignettes because coherent text is easier to memorise than disconnected phrases, but a few remain. Sometimes we can even find a scene in transition, one that has been partially converted to a coherent dialogue but still retains some disconnected phrases.

The portions of the Colloquia that remain as disconnected phrases are, interestingly, overwhelmingly concerned with unpleasant situations; perhaps ancient teachers were less keen to produce coherent scenes involving such situations than to describe more positive interactions.

6.1 PREFACE TO THE PHRASEBOOK

The main surviving phrasebook is preceded by a short preface (Colloquium Harleianum 11a–b), which separates it from the school scenes that precede and alerts the reader not to try to make coherent sense out of the disconnected phrases.

> Here I shall give you a collection of assorted useful phrases. They include the greeting portion of conversations, questions, insults, and many other things.

6.2 A SELECTION OF EXCUSES

This passage (Colloquium Harleianum 15e–g) shows a phrasebook section in the process of transition to a coherent scene. Its main feature is a list of excuses for not doing something immediately; some of these excuses look a bit feeble today, but they were probably more convincing in antiquity. The list of excuses is preceded by a short dialogue introducing the type of situation in which one might want to use them. This dialogue may not be an original feature of the passage, as not every section of the phrasebook has one. It would have been easier to memorise than the list of excuses that followed, and therefore successive users of this book would have been tempted to extend the dialogue at the expense of the list; that type of expansion and contraction probably explains the creation of many of the coherent scenes in the Eastern portions of the Colloquia.

> FRIEND 1: You did promptly what I asked you to do, didn't you?
> FRIEND 2: Actually I haven't done it yet.
> FRIEND 1: Why not?
> FRIEND 2: I'm going to do it in a little while, because now I'm in a hurry to go out / I'm hungry / I'm on my way to a wedding / I'm on my way to see a friend / my friends are waiting for me / I'm on my way to take a bath.

6.3 A SELECTION OF INSULTS AND OTHER PHRASES TO USE IN ARGUMENTS

The insults section (Colloquium Harleianum 16a–18j, 24a–e) is one of the longest and most detailed portions of the phrasebook. Its presence demonstrates that an ancient phrasebook was not intended to function as a reference work, the way a modern one often does: in the heat of an argument it is simply impractical to stop and look up a crushing insult, because slow communication during which one can pause to look things up depends on the sympathetic co-operation of the other person in the dialogue. A phrasebook with an extensive collection of insults must have been material that the writer expected the user to memorise before needing it, for a long list of insults can only be of use to a language learner if memorised in advance.

> Get out of here!
> Why are you standing around?
> What business is it of yours – are you my overseer?
> Go away, impostor!
> Are you insulting me, you baleful and hateful man?

Do this to them, shameless one!

Shut up!

Goodbye, you worthless man.

Your master will hear about this if he encounters me!

Let go! Look what you're doing to me!

I don't care about your threats!

I avenge any insults I receive, so you have no hope at all.

Keep your hands over there!

Oh dear, are you going to beat me? I am afraid, because your status is high.

I could beat you, but I won't, out of respect for you and for the gods.

Are you insulting me, scoundrel? May you be crucified!

You behave badly and do not even know that it doesn't do you any good.

Why? Because I am a free-born man, and you are a useless slave.

Be quiet!

So you want to learn at last: the lesson is that I am not like you.

You aren't, impostor?

I want to find out whether you are a slave or a freedman.

I won't give you an explanation.

Why not?

Because you don't deserve one.

Let's go to your master.

Maybe.

I am a well-born man known to everyone, and the master of a household.

Yeah, one can really see that by looking at you!

Let's go!

*****

Does that man, who is fit only to fight beasts in the arena, insult me? Let me go, and I'll shake out all his teeth!

I shall blind you!

I see what you're doing to me.

I'll make you go to prison, where you deserve to spend the rest of your life.

Are you insulting me, gaoler?

> You and I are equal: I don't care about you.
> You have a friend, but so do I.
> You speak well. Look, I yield to you.

Some of the insults look very similar to modern ones, but others now seem strange. Many ancient insults are based on the social stratification of a slave-owning culture: calling a free-born man a slave, or even a freedman, was a serious affront of a type simply not available in our culture. There were many subtle ways of delivering this affront; for example 'I want to find out whether you are a slave or a freedman' is probably intended to be spoken to a free-born man and carries its insult in the implicit assumption that the person addressed cannot possibly be free-born. Likewise 'Your master will hear about this if he encounters me' could be a threat to a slave, but as such it is distinctly feeble: if the speaker actually knows who the slave's master is, a threat to go and tell him about the altercation would be more effective than a threat dependent on a chance meeting that may not occur, and if the speaker does not know who the slave's master is, it is unlikely that he will find out by meeting him. As an insult to a free man, however, this statement is excellent because of its implicit assumption that the person addressed must be a slave.

The insults are an interesting mixture of expressions taken from literary sources and ones current in the language of the empire; the collection may originally have been formed from a variety of sources. A few conciliatory remarks are included ('your status is high', 'look, I yield to you'), for the benefit of readers who preferred not to escalate a conflict.

For another selection of insults, see the Pompeiian graffiti in chapter 11.2.

CHAPTER 7

Lunch Time

Many of the Colloquia describe two lunches: the lunch of the school-boy in the first section (see the ends of passages 2.2 and 2.7 above) and that of an adult in the second. The child's lunch is fairly simple, but the adult's can be elaborate. And while the child actually consumes his lunch, the adult lunch scenes never describe the eating of the meal, only the preparations for it. The reason is probably that the phrases and vocabulary needed for eating lunch are largely the same as those needed for eating dinner, which are provided in the dinner scenes (see passages 9.2–9.5), and the writer did not want to duplicate this material.

7.1 FURTHER READING

For more information on Roman meals, see the works listed in the introduction to chapter 9; for commentary on the passages below see Dickey (2012–15).

7.2 PREPARING FOR A GUEST

This dialogue (Colloquia Monacensia–Einsidlensia 7a–9o) reveals the mechanics of having a guest to lunch, from the initial invitation to the moment the guest appears.

HOST: Hey, Gaius, where are you off to?
GAIUS: I'm on my way home, and I'm in a hurry; why do you ask?
HOST: Would you like to have a little lunch with me today?
We have good wine from our own estate.
GAIUS: Definitely!
HOST: Then be sure to show up at the right time.
GAIUS: Just send a slave round when you want me to come; I'll be at home.

HOST: Agreed! (*to slave*) You, boy, follow me to the butcher's shop; let's buy something for lunch. Ask him how much the fish is.

SELLER: Ten denarii.

HOST (*to slave*): You, boy, carry it home, so that the rest of us can go to the greengrocer's shop and buy vegetables, which we need, and fruit: mulberries, figs, peaches, pears, and azaroles. (*to second slave*) There, you have got everything we bought: carry it home. (*to other slaves, on returning home*) Someone call the cook! Where is he?

SLAVE: He went upstairs.

HOST: What does he want up there? Tell him to come down here! (*to cook*) Take these things and cook them carefully, to make a nice lunch for us. (*to another slave*) Take this key, open the casket, and get out the key to the cellar. Unlock the cellar and bring up the things we need: salt, Spanish oil, oil for the lamps, fish-sauce (both the first-class and the second-class varieties), sharp vinegar, white wine, black wine, new wine, old wine, dry firewood, coals, a burning ember, an axe, serving vessels, dishes, pots, a grid-iron, a cover, a mortar and pestle, and a knife.

SLAVE: What else do you want?

HOST: Only this, boy: go to Gaius and say to him, 'Come, let's have lunch before we go to the baths.' Go, run, do it quickly, not so slowly! Immediately! (*when the slave returns*) Have you been to Gaius?

SLAVE: Yes.

HOST: Where was he?

SLAVE: He was sitting at home.

HOST: And what was he doing?

SLAVE: He was studying.

HOST: And what did he say?

SLAVE: He said, 'I'm waiting for my friends; I'll follow them when they get here.'

HOST: Well, go back to him and say, 'Everyone is already here!' Bring him back with you. (*to others*) You lot, meanwhile, set out the glasses and the bronze vessels carefully. Put out cushions in the dining room, and throw water outside the front door. Go on, move!

SLAVES (*later*): We have now prepared the dining room; everything's ready.

HOST: And Gaius still isn't here? Go and find him and say,
    'You're making us have lunch late!'
SLAVE: Look, here he is; he was just coming.
HOST: Go and meet him, bring him in! Gaius, why are you
    standing outside instead of coming in?

The invitation is given in person by the host, spontaneously or apparently spontaneously; this practice was more common in Roman
culture than it is today, but we also have some written invitations
from antiquity (see *T.Vindol.* 11.291 in chapter 11.3 and *P.Oxy.* VI.926
in chapter 11.4). The host then goes shopping for the meal.

The shopping is performed with a retinue of slaves (cf. passage 4.4),
so that the initial, highly perishable purchase can be sent home quickly
via a slave and other(s) remain to carry the remaining purchases.
The food involved is still familiar today, apart from azaroles, which
are exotic fruits resembling cherries.

Upon arriving home the host hands the food over to his cook, with
instructions to prepare it well, and then orders slaves to ready the
dining room and fetch supplies from the cellar. The cellar is kept
locked, to make sure the slaves do not steal food from it; the large,
heavy cellar key is kept in a casket that is in turn secured with a smaller
lock whose key can more conveniently be carried on the owner's
person. The condiments necessary for the meal include fish sauce
(garum, a salty liquid made from aged fish that was ubiquitous in
Roman cooking) and four kinds of wine ('black' wine was a common

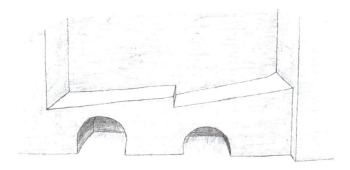

FIG. 31 Stands for selling fish in the Roman market hall (*macellum*) in Naples, Italy:
the sloping tables allowed easy drainage when cleaning fish

FIG. 32 Stand of a vegetable seller as depicted on a second-century terracotta relief
from the Isola Sacra necropolis, now in the Museo Ostiense, Ostia, Italy

ancient term for what we would call red wine). Utensils mentioned
include the materials for making a fire in a brazier in the dining room
(the axe would be used for cutting wood to burn and the burning
ember, which would have been taken from a fire already lit elsewhere
in the house, is for lighting the fire). This fire warmed the room for the
diners; other fires were sometimes used for heating wine and food that
was served hot.

The cushions are for the guests to recline on; the dining room is
equipped with three permanent masonry couches, so these do not need

FIG. 33 Brazier made of bronze and iron, first century, found at Pompeii and now in the National Archaeological Museum, Naples, Italy (partly restored); the handles make it possible to carry the brazier while lit without burning one's hands on the hot underside

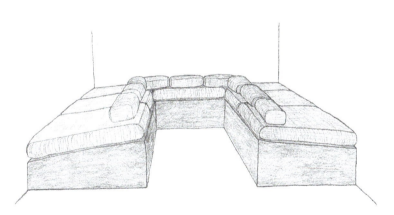

FIG. 34 Triclinium dining room with masonry couches and cushions set up ready for a meal (reconstruction at Xanten Archaeological Park, Germany); the food would have been served on a small table in the central well

FIG. 35 Reclining banqueter as depicted on the first-century gravestone of Gaius
Julius Baccus in the Romano-Germanic Museum in Cologne, Germany (inv. Stein
24); notice the little table with cups and the attendant, who is depicted in a smaller
scale to indicate his lesser importance, waiting to serve as needed

to be adjusted but do need padding to make them comfortable.
The guests will recline on their left elbows and eat with one hand
from pre-cut food placed on a small table in their midst. The glass and
bronze vessels suggest a fairly well-endowed household, but not one at
the very top end of the social hierarchy: poorer people used tableware

FIG. 36 Roman glass tableware made at Cologne in the third and fourth centuries and now in the Romano-Germanic Museum in Cologne, Germany

made of pottery or wood, while the richest families used silver. The purpose of throwing water outside was probably to dampen the packed earth in front of the house and prevent clouds of dust arising when the guests arrived.

In the midst of all these preparations messengers are sent repeatedly to Gaius, urging him to come; his failure to respond, and indeed the lack of any agreement on a precise time for his arrival, seems surprising in a modern context, but Gaius finally appears at exactly the moment when the meal is actually ready. Modern hosts and hostesses, having asked guests to arrive at a pre-arranged hour, often find themselves frantically trying to get the cooking and cleaning ready in what turns out to be too little time, while guests can find it embarrassing to have to work out whether it would be more polite to turn up at the agreed time or somewhat later – and if later, how much later. The ancient system of repeated messages sent by slaves, as described in this passage, is labour-intensive (though that may not matter much if the host has plenty of slaves) and works only if the guest lives fairly close to the host, but within those constraints it appears to have been an efficient and successful system of causing the guest to show up exactly when the meal was actually ready. It was not, however, universally employed during the empire, for although the written invitation in *T. Vindol.* 11.291 does not mention a time, the one in *P. Oxy.* VI.926 does.

7.3 A CELEBRATORY MEAL

This passage (Colloquium Montepessulanum 10a–13a), describing lunch offered to a lawyer in gratitude for his help in securing success in a lawsuit (cf. section 5 above), contains many elements resembling the previous passage. The household is, however, a richer one, for the table holds silver vessels rather than bronze.

> The judge has come, the lawsuit is over, and we have won. Since you brought me success with your help, I invite you to lunch today. Please come! (*to kitchen staff*) Since I have invited friends here for a meal, come and prepare everything that is necessary, and tell the cook to season the food well. (*to other slaves*) Come here, fluff up the cushions, set the pillows out in the dining room, drape covers over the couches, sweep the floor, throw water outside, arrange the dining room, bring the cups and the silverware. You, boy, pick up the flask and fetch water, split wood for burning, wipe off the table, and put it in the middle of the room. I shall bring out the wine myself. Wash the cups. The food has now been delivered; let it be cooked.

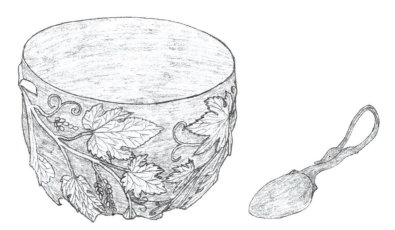

FIG. 37 Roman silver cup (first century, partly restored) and spoon, now in the British Museum (inv. GR 1867.5–8.1410 and GR 1913.5–31.7)

CHAPTER 8

Afternoons at the Baths

Bathing in the Roman world was not simply about cleanliness; it was the main recreational opportunity of the day. Although country villas usually had their own bath-houses, in cities everyone used the public facilities, which were far better than an individual household could have provided.

Bathing was a social activity: Romans went to the baths as groups of friends or family (cf. the arrangements made in passage 5.4 above) and met other people there (not always in positive ways; again cf. passage 5.4). The larger bath complexes had extensive exercise facilities; in a crowded urban environment these might be the only places available for ordinary people to stretch their legs, play games, and relax.

FIG. 38 Caldarium of the reconstructed baths at Xanten Archaeological Park, Germany

Admission to these exercise areas might even be free, for the (small) charge for admission to the baths was sometimes paid only when the bather entered the first of the rooms containing heat and/or water.

Everyone went to the baths: men, women, children, noblemen, freedmen, and slaves. At some facilities everyone bathed together, but at others the genders were segregated. Some baths had completely separate facilities for men and women, and at others the afternoon, when high-ranking men would have finished their public business, was reserved for a males-only bathing session, with a females-only session earlier in the day. Often the baths were crowded and noisy; see Seneca's description in his letter 56.1–2 (quoted in chapter 11.6).

The bathing process was normally conducted in a fixed order. First the bathers undressed in the *apodyterium* (undressing room) and left their clothes with a servant they had brought for the purpose or one hired at the baths. Poorer bathers were obliged to leave their clothes unattended, but this was undesirable as clothing (which, as it all had to be made by hand, had significant value) was sometimes stolen from baths.

Exercise, if it was included (something not feasible in the smaller bath-houses), came immediately after undressing: ancient clothing was not ideally suited to strenuous activity, as well as difficult to replace if damaged, so nudity was the preferred condition for exercise, at least in warm regions. The options available for exercise might include wrestling, boxing, weight-lifting, and various ball games; often a large open area (*palaestra*) was available for exercise, but some types of game could also be played in indoor facilities, which were particularly desirable in colder climates.

The bathers then proceeded to the first room of the baths proper. This was the *tepidarium*, a warm room where bathers adjusted to the warm temperature and were anointed with olive oil. Next came a hot room, where they sat and sweated; at larger baths there might be several different types of hot room involving different types of heat, but bathers normally visited only one of these on any given day; the primary term for a hot room was *caldarium*. Once a sufficient sweat had been generated, bathers immersed themselves in the hot pool, a receptacle large enough to hold several bathers but not large enough to swim in (often around three meters long, two meters wide, and one meter deep). They then sometimes returned to the *tepidarium* to re-adjust to cooler temperatures (this phase is not attested in the

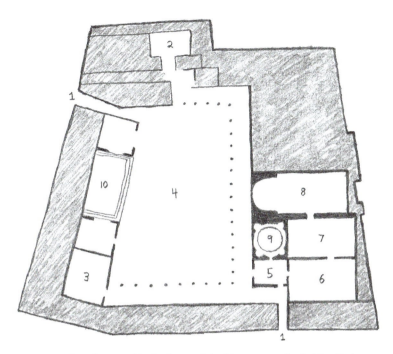

FIG. 39 Plan of a typical bath: the men's bathing areas at the Stabian Baths at Pompeii (first century). Entrances are at 1, toilets at 2, *apodyterium* at 3, palaestra (exercise area) at 4, vestibule of baths proper (where payment could be taken) at 5, a second *apodyterium* (for those who did not exercise) at 6, *tepidarium* at 7, *caldarium* at 8, *frigidarium* at 9, open-air pool at 10. Shaded areas include the women's bath complex, service areas, and shops.

Colloquia) before bathing in a cold pool, either in an indoor *frigidarium* or in an outdoor swimming pool. Then they were dried off with towels, got dressed, and returned home.

8.1 FURTHER READING

For further information on Roman bathing see Fagan (1999, on the social aspects of bathing), Nielsen (1990, on the buildings used, which are now among the best-preserved Roman remains), Yegül (1992, also on the buildings, and 2010, on the cultural phenomenon), and Dickey (2012–15, commentary on the passages quoted below).

8.2 A FAMILY OUTING

This bathing scene (Colloquia Monacensia–Einsidlensia 10a–u) shows a father taking his son to the baths.

> FATHER: Take the towels down to the bath, and the strigil, face-cloth, foot-cloth, flask of oil, and soap. Go ahead of us and hold a place for us.
>
> SLAVES: Which baths shall we go to? The state baths or a private one?
>
> FATHER: You choose – but go on ahead of us, you folk who are here. Make sure there's hot water ready when we arrive; I'll send someone to tell you when we're coming.
>
> FATHER (*later, to his young son*): Get up, let's go! Do you want to go from here through the portico, because of the rain? And do you want to come to the toilet?
>
> SON: That's a good idea; I need to go.
>
> FATHER (*when finished in the toilet*): Now let's go. (*on arrival in the changing rooms, to son*) Take off your clothes. (*to slaves*) Take off my shoes, put our clothes together, cover them up, and watch them well. Don't doze off, because there are thieves here. (*to son*) Grab a ball for us; let's play in the ball-court.
>
> SON: I want to practise in the wrestling-ground. Come on, it's been ages since we wrestled; let's do it just for a minute.
>
> FATHER: Well, I don't know whether I can. I gave up wrestling a long time ago – but okay, if you want, I'll give it a try. (*After a very short bout*) That's all I can manage; I'm exhausted. Let's go into the first room of the baths, the warm room. Give the bath-keeper these coins and get the change.
>
> SON (*once in the warm room*): Rub oil on me!
>
> FATHER: I've done it; now I need to put some on myself.
>
> SON: Come on, rub!
>
> FATHER: Come along to the sweat room. (*later*) Are you sweating now?
>
> SON: Definitely; in fact I've had all I can take.
>
> FATHER: Let's go on to the hot pool. Go down here.
>
> SON: Let's use the dry heat room and go down to the hot pool that way.

FATHER (*later*): Right, go on down, and then pour hot water over me. Now it's time to get out and jump into the outside pool. Swim!

SON (*later*): I've done it.

FATHER: Go over to the basin and pour some water over yourself.

SON: I've done it.

FATHER (*to slaves*): Hand me the strigil, and rub me down. Wrap the towels around me, dry my head and feet. Give me my shoes, and put them on me. Hand me my undergarment, mantle, and Dalmatian tunic. Gather up the clothes and all our things. Follow me home, stopping at the bath-shop to buy us some chopped food, boiled lupin seeds, and pickled beans.

BATH ATTENDANT (*to family on their way out*): I hope you had a good bath, and may all be well for you!

The excursion begins (as always with bath scenes in the Colloquia) with instructions to the slaves who carried towels and other items needed for bathing. Here the slaves are also instructed to enter the bathing rooms proper, which were often crowded, wait until seats became free, and sit in them until the family party arrived: this was the only way that the family could be sure of getting seats without having to wait.

FIG. 40 A bathing party, as depicted on a fourth-century mosaic at Piazza Armerina, Sicily: three bathers (the three central figures, perhaps a mother and her sons) are accompanied by two slave girls. One slave carries a box of textiles, probably towels and/or clean clothes; the other carries a box and bag with the smaller bathing implements.

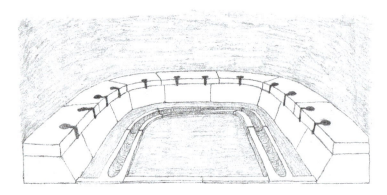

FIG. 41 Twelve-seater public toilet in the third-century Bath of the Cyclopes at Dougga, Tunisia

The question is then raised of which bathing establishment to use; most large towns had more than one, and in the later empire Rome had nearly a thousand. The state facilities (*thermae*) were the largest and offered more recreational opportunities than the privately-owned baths (*balneae*), which might only provide a few small rooms' worth of facilities. All were open to the public on payment of a small fee. Which type of establishment these bathers end up at is not completely clear: the fact that they exercise points to a state bath, but the instructions to make sure there is hot water ready by the time the party arrives suggests a smaller facility. It is possible that the writer, wishing to provide readers with all the phrases they would need for either kind of bath, deliberately included mutually exclusive possibilities.

The writer is certainly taking care to cover all the aspects of the bathing experience. He even gets in a visit to the public toilets, which were often located near the entrance to the baths. Going to the toilet was, like bathing, a communal activity for Romans; the toilets consisted simply of a row of holes in a long bench, with no privacy whatsoever.

The bathers then undress, leaving a slave to guard their clothes from thieves, and start to exercise; the writer adroitly fits in the words for the multiple exercise options available by having the bathers discuss whether to wrestle or play ball. The father, who is out of shape, can

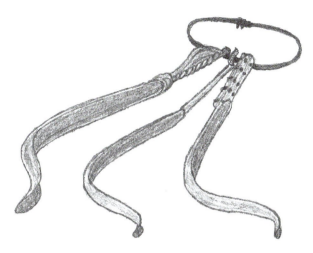

FIG. 42 Set of bronze strigils, first to third century, found at Cologne and now in the Romano-Germanic Museum in Cologne, Germany

only manage a small amount of exercise, and then he and his son pay the entrance fee and enter the main section of the baths. They go through the rooms in order, with the writer again managing to squeeze in more possibilities than any one bather would take advantage of by including a discussion of which hot room to use.

The end of the bathing procedure includes a surprising detail: the bathers take a shower by pouring water over themselves and then scrape themselves with a strigil before being dried with towels. The strigil was a curved metal scraper; it was normally used directly after exercising, to scrape off dirt and sweat (cf. Philogelos joke 150 in chapter 11.1). The bathers may have used the strigil this way before entering the first room of the baths, but that is not stated explicitly; what is stated is that it is used at the end of the procedure, when the bathers have immersed themselves in two pools of water and ought to be completely clean.

The reason for the scraping is that immersion in the water of a Roman bath did not always lead to cleanliness. The pools were crowded with people who had just exercised and covered themselves with oil; even if those people all used a strigil before entering the water, the water would have become dirty very fast, and it was not changed frequently (cf. Philogelos joke 163 in chapter 11.1 and Martial epigram

14.51 in chapter 11.5). Under these circumstances one would naturally want to take a shower and use a strigil at the end of the bathing process.

Finally the bathers are dried and dressed (by slaves, since they belong to a level of society in which they could not be expected to do such things for themselves). They wear Dalmatian tunics, the garment with long, full sleeves worn by the woman in the centre of the bathing party in figure 40 and by her two slaves. Then the bathers set off for home, fortified for the trip by snacks from one of the shops at the baths. As they leave, the bath attendant gives them one of the ritual compliments associated with the bathing experience. There were two of these compliments: on the way in to the baths it was customary to say to a bather *bene lava* 'Have a good bath!', and as bathers departed the compliment was *salvum lavisse* or *salvum lotum* (literally 'healthy and washed'). These phrases were such a fundamental part of the bathing experience that when later conquests turned the public baths of the Eastern empire into the Arabic *hammam*, the compliments survived (in Arabic translation) and are still used today in some regions.

FIG. 43 Mosaic at the entrance to the tepidarium of a Roman bath in Timgad, Algeria (partly restored); this was positioned so that bathers entering the complex were greeted with *bene lava* and those leaving with *salvu(m) lavisse*. Note the bathing sandals, for which see passage 8.3.

8.3 INSTRUCTIONS TO SLAVES

This version of the bathing scene (Colloquium Celtis 55a–64b) is cast almost entirely as a series of orders to slaves. Issuing such orders was often the only way to get things done in antiquity, for most people were prevented by both custom and practicality from doing basic things for themselves. Modern travellers may have linguistic difficulties checking into a hotel room, but once in the room they are unlikely to need further language skills: they can flip a switch to turn on the light, use a tap to get hot water, and find the towels on the towel rack. But the ancient traveller with similar needs had to ask someone to light a lamp, heat water, and bring towels. This bathing scene, therefore, gives Latin learners the phrases they would need to negotiate the baths successfully.

BATHER: Get yourself ready faster, so that we can bathe sooner. Carry down to the baths our things and our changes of clothes and our bathing sandals. Put them out for us carefully, and hold good places for us, so that we can have a pleasant time. Come on – you'll get a scolding if you don't get a move on. You, go on ahead with the flask of oil. Why are you so slow? Pick up this stuff and carry it! . . .

I entered the anointing-room and asked for a flask of oil.

BATHER: Give me oil, anoint me, and rub my whole body all over. Now let's go on in. I've sweated a lot already; let's go to the hot tub. Stand back: I want to jump in. Turn on the tap and add more water. Let's go outside to the pool, and let me jump in so I can swim. Give me the strigil and scrape me down. Give me the towels, and dry my head and shoulders, chest and stomach, hands and sides, back and thighs, knees and shins, feet and heels, and the soles of my feet. Now go and dress yourselves properly, and give me my clothes so that I can get dressed. Dry my friend and dress him, so he can come with me.

BATH ATTENDANT: I hope you had a good bath! . . . Farewell, sir, and may all be well for you.

BATHER: Collect our things, and whatever else we need, and follow me; let's go home. This is a good bath with really hot water; I thank the bath attendant.

The items listed as needing to be taken to the baths in this passage are largely different from those in the previous passage. In addition to clean clothes to put on after the bath, the bathers here bring special bathing sandals. These sandals, which had extra-thick soles, protected bathers' feet from the heat of the floors in the hot rooms of the baths (notice how in figure 40 the bathers wear sandals and the slaves do not; note also the sandals as emblematic of baths in figure 43). The hot rooms were usually heated by means of hypocaust floors, that is, floors heated from underneath by hot air from a furnace; in order to get the air in the room hot enough to cause a good sweat, it was often necessary to make the floor uncomfortably hot, so bathing could not easily be done barefoot.

At the end of the bath sequence these bathers again use a strigil, but this time a shower is not mentioned. In describing the drying process the writer seizes the opportunity to teach the words for the different parts of the body, neatly arranging them in order from top to bottom.

FIG. 44 The final stages of a bath, as depicted on a fourth-century mosaic (from an apse, hence the distorted perspective) at Piazza Armerina, Sicily: a young man who has recently bathed is wrapped in towels and dried by a slave, while another stands ready to dress him.

8.4 A DELUXE EXPERIENCE

The bather depicted in this passage (Colloquium Montepessulanum 13g–16e) is extravagant. On arrival at the baths, he buys twenty portions of top-quality ointment and frankincense, a highly valuable substance normally offered to the gods. Exactly what he does with his purchases is not explicitly stated, but the context suggests that the ointment, at least, is immediately used by the bather and his friends.

MASTER: What time is it?

SERVANT: It is now the eighth hour.

MASTER: Tell someone to go to the Tigilline baths and announce that I'm coming there. Follow us – I'm talking to you, scum! (*in the changing room*) Guard our clothes carefully. Now, you go and find us a good place, and I'll get something to anoint us with. (*to ointment seller*) Hello, Julius! Sell me frankincense and ointment, top quality, enough for twenty people today. (*once inside the baths, to slave*) Boy, take off my shoes. Take my clothes, give me oil, anoint me. (*to friends*) Let's go on in. (*after a spell in the hot room*) Have you sweated yet?

FRIEND: Yes!

MASTER: Give me the soap, rub me. The water in the hot tub is just the right temperature. (*later*) Now let's go outside and swim in the pool. (*later*) That was a good, cold swim! Now give me the strigil, scrape me with it. Give me the towels and dry me off. Put on my shoes, give me my clothes, and let me get dressed. . . .

BATH ATTENDANT (*as the party departs*): I hope you had a good bath, sir!

The location of the bathing is specified as the Tigilline baths; these were a real establishment, located in Rome and probably constructed in the first century AD. Identifying the baths by name is very unusual in the Colloquia, which normally offer a generic template without naming any real places or people. The time is also specified, as the eighth hour (around 2 p.m.: see the explanation of passage 3.3 and

FIG. 45 Glass oil flask with bronze lid attached to handle by braided wire, first century (found at Pompeii and now in the National Archaeological Museum in Naples, Italy)

Martial epigram 4.8 in chapter 11.5); this was the most popular hour for men's bathing, though women often bathed earlier.

Note the use of soap, which is rarely mentioned in discussions of the bathing process. It appears to be rubbed on the bather before he gets into the hot tub and would no doubt have compounded the problem of dirty water.

CHAPTER 9

Dinners

Having guests to dinner was an important part of Roman social life and is described in detail in several of the Colloquia. Dining is also extensively depicted in mainstream literature (e.g. Petronius), so to a certain extent the Colloquia are less important here than in other areas. Nevertheless they offer important insights by considering dinner parties from angles not normally seen elsewhere, such as the preparation involved in giving a party. The Colloquia also remind us that not every Roman dinner was a party; sometimes a Roman came home by himself, ate a simple meal, and went to bed.

9.1 FURTHER READING

For further information on Roman dining see Dunbabin (2003, an excellent collection and discussion of ancient depictions of dinners), Grocock and Grainger (2006, an accessible translation of the Roman cookbook bearing the name of Apicius), Salza Prina Ricotti (1995, a collection of Roman recipes adapted for modern use), Thurmond (2006, an interesting explanation of Roman food production and preservation processes), Dalby (2003, providing brief explanations of nearly all Roman foods and drinks), Cool (2006, a comprehensive study of food and drink in Roman Britain, based primarily on archaeological evidence), Roller (2006, an examination of the convention of reclining for meals), and Slater (1991, a collection of studies of various aspects of dining culture in both Greece and Rome).

9.2 PREPARATIONS FOR A BIG DINNER

Roman hosts made an effort to provide food that was not only tasty but also interesting and varied, served in a pleasant environment; by modern standards some ancient dinner parties went over the top in pursuing these aims. An elaborate dinner required extensive preparation, and although the actual work of preparation would be done by slaves, a good host took an active part in directing it.

The passage below (Colloquium Celtis 47a–54b) is slightly garbled as a result of conflation of what must originally have been several different dinner preparation scenes. Nevertheless one can see the general outlines of the process clearly. The dining room has to be got ready by cleaning it, making a fire to warm it, setting up couches for diners to recline on and covering them with cloths and cushions, laying out the tableware and candlesticks, and spreading flowers. Food needs to be brought out of the store-room and prepared; the writer has probably let his urge to teach extra vocabulary run away with him somewhat here, for the number of different foods mentioned is so great that even a Roman dinner party would have been most unlikely to offer them all. (In any case many of the foods mentioned do not keep and would therefore not have been in the store-room to begin with.) The passage has much in common with the lunch preparation scenes in passages 7.2 and 7.3.

> Tell the other servants that I shall need to have something to eat after the bath. Set out a kettle and lots of pots, make dinner, put coals in the dining-room brazier, sweep the house, bring water. Set up the couch and put the coverings on it. Open up the store-room and bring out wine, oil, fish-sauce, and beer; for spices pepper, silphium juice, cumin, mixed spices, salt; onion and garlic, cabbages and leeks, beet greens and mallows, eggs and asparagus, nuts and beans, plums and pears, fruits and lupins, artichokes and hyacinth bulbs, radishes and turnips, salad and salted fish, rice and barley-gruel, porridge and peas, beans; vinegar and unmixed wine, fish and gourds, a bit of pork and of suckling pig, salted meat, a little bit of bacon, little fruits, sea-kales, a jug full of absinth-flavoured wine, and another jug of spiced wine. Bring out cups, a bowl, and a candlestick; decorate the three-legged table, sprinkle flowers in the dining room, put out coals and incense, have everything ready. Tell the other servants that they

should make tasty foods, since my guests are distinguished men and foreigners.

The foods mentioned include many that were commonly used in Roman cookery (including fish sauce, for which see above on passage 7.2; pepper, which is mentioned 452 times in Apicius' cookbook; cumin, and onions). Others, including rice, would have been considered exotic. The term 'silphium juice' originally referred to the resin of a fennel-like plant that grew wild in Libya, but owing to overexploitation that plant became extinct long before this passage was written; in the Empire the word went on being used but was applied to a different condiment, a resin from central Asia known as asafoetida. The gourds, a cheap food often fed to slaves, were similar to our marrows; sea-kales were a cabbage-like plant that grew near the sea.

FIG. 46 Pottery wine jug with built-in strainer, first century (Xanten Archaeological Park, Germany)

FIG. 47 Roman bronze candlestick, second or third century, found in Cologne and
now in the Romano-Germanic Museum in Cologne, Germany (inv. 24.403)

9.3 A DINNER PARTY

This passage (Colloquia Monacensia–Einsidlensia 11a–12a) describes
a dinner party from the guests' arrival to their departure.

> *As guests arrive and gather in an anteroom for drinks before dinner:*
> HOST (*to slaves*): Put the chairs here, and the seats, the bench,
> the couch that seats two, and the cushions. (*to guest*) Do sit
> down!
> GUEST: I shall.
> HOST (*to slave*): Why are you just standing there? Rinse out a cup
> and mix a drink with hot water: I'm very thirsty. Mix some for

everyone. (*to guests*) Who wants what? Spiced wine or sweet boiled wine? (*to slave*) Mix him exactly what he asked for. (*to guest*) How about you, what would you like? (*to slave*) Rinse out another cup.

GUEST: Mix me a hot drink: don't make it boiling or lukewarm, but just right, and pour me a little bit of it to taste. (*after tasting*) Put in some fresh water. (*after tasting again*) Add more wine.

Once drinks have been distributed and the group moves into the dining room:

HOST: Why are you all standing up? Do be seated, if you'd like to!

GUEST: Yes, let's recline for dinner. Tell us where you want us to be.

HOST: You should take the place of honour. (*to slaves*) Bring out the fish-sauce prepared with water, and let us taste the boiled mallows. Hand me a napkin. Bring on the food. Put some fish-sauce made with oil into the vinegar cup. Divide up the pigs' trotters, and cut up the pig's stomach and the boiled tripe. (*to guest*) Will you have some pepper dressing? Dip it in this.

GUEST: I shall!

HOST: Yes, do! (*to slaves*) Give us some tender fig-fattened liver, thrushes, sweetbreads, lettuces. One of you break the bread and put it in a basket; pass it around to everyone. (*to guests*) Eat, friends! ... (*to slaves*) Give us salted fish, pilchards, beans, a cabbage sprout with fish-sauce and Spanish oil, meat in grated turnip, a roast chicken, pieces of meat in sauce, slices of meat, roast suckling pig. Put out the platter with endives, radishes, mint, white olives, freshly salted cheese, truffles, and mushrooms.

When the meal is over and the guests are ready to move on to drinking:

HOST: Give dinner to the servants and to the cook; and give him dessert too, because he did a good job. Bring water for our hands, and wipe off the table. ... Give us cups and wine. Let's drink fresh water from the cooler.

GUEST: Mix me some hot wine.

SLAVE: In a big cup?

GUEST: Preferably in a smaller one.

SLAVE: Certainly.

GUEST: I'm hoping to try more than one drink this evening!

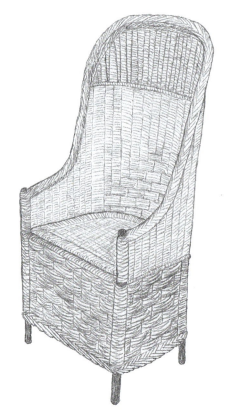

FIG. 48 Roman wicker chair (reconstruction at Xanten Archaeological
Park, Germany)

GUEST 1: If you will allow me, I drink to you; will you allow this?

GUEST 2: When it comes from you, I'm honoured!

HOST: Why aren't you drinking? Come on, sir, have something
to drink!

GUEST: I haven't got anything to drink – I asked for wine and no-
one gave me any.

HOST (*to slaves*): Give us sweet cheesecakes.

GUESTS: Let's go home now; we've had enough. (*to slave*) Light
the torch.

SLAVE: Here it is.

GUESTS: You have entertained us well.

HOST (*to slave, after the guests have left*): Boy, come here, collect all
these things and put them back where they belong.

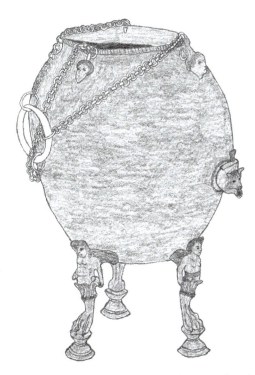

FIG. 49 Water heater for use in a dining room, third century, found at Kaiseraugst and now in the Augusta Raurica Museum in Augst, Switzerland (inv. 1974.10376)

On arrival the guests gather in a library or similar room for pre-dinner drinks; in this room they sit upright on chairs and benches, rather than reclining as in the dining room. When the guests arrive, therefore, the host has slaves bring the necessary furniture and invites the guests to be seated before directing the slaves to offer them drinks.

Unlike Greeks, who mixed wine and water in a large communal bowl and dispensed portions of the mixture to everyone from that bowl, Roman hosts provided their guests with individually mixed drinks. A wide range of possibilities was available: the variable elements included not only the amount and type of wine, but also the temperature of the water. Cold beverages could be produced using snow (which in some regions had to be imported at vast expense), and hot ones were made using water from a special hot-water dispenser in the

FIG. 50 Diners reclining on couches, as depicted on a first-century wall painting in the House of the Chaste Lovers at Pompeii, Italy

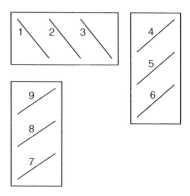

FIG. 51 One common seating plan for Roman dinners: nine diners (represented here by diagonal lines) recline on three couches. The host takes place 9, with other members of his family occupying the other places on his couch (7 and 8); the guests take the other two couches, with the place of honour being 1, that closest to the host, and descending in order from there.

room. Before dispensing a hot beverage a good waiter would rinse out the cup with hot water to warm it so that it would not cool down the drink. Because the actual mixing was done by slaves, not by the host, guests could insist that a drink be prepared exactly to their liking without being perceived as rude.

The party then moves into the dining room, where they recline on couches. The couches were arranged in a predictable order, and

FIG. 52 Loaf of bread carbonised by the eruption of Vesuvius in the first century; the baker's stamp indicates that the bread was made by Celer, the slave of Quintus Granius Verus (*fecit Q. Grani Veri s. Celer*). Found at Herculaneum and now in the National Archaeological Museum, Naples, Italy (inv. 84596).

some places were considered better than others; the host therefore indicates who is to have which place. He then asks the slaves to bring on the dinner, which comes in multiple courses. As in the previous passage, the writer's desire to include as much food vocabulary as possible may have artificially expanded the number of different dishes on offer.

The foods mentioned include pigs' trotters, a pig's stomach, and boiled tripe. These portions of meat were much more highly regarded in antiquity than they are now: the trotters and stomach both appear in Apicius' high-class cookbook (for the stomach, see the recipes in chapter 11.7). The bread is not cut, but broken into pieces along lines incised by the baker before putting the bread in the oven; many such incised loaves have been found at Pompeii and Herculaneum.

When the guests have eaten all they can, the cook and waiters are allowed to have the leftovers; this privilege is evidently not to be taken for granted, as it is justified here on the grounds that they did a good job with the meal. The cook (but not the waiters) is

FIG. 53 Row of slaves offering drinks, as depicted on a fourth- or fifth-century
mosaic from the House of Bacchus at Complutum, Spain

also allowed to have dessert. The waiters cannot immediately avail
themselves of the opportunity to eat, however, since they first need
to clear away the remains of the meal, wipe down the tables, and
bring water for the diners to wash their hands. Romans did not
have forks and ate largely with their fingers, and much of their
food was served in thick sauces, so despite the napkins mentioned
earlier in the scene the diners' hands probably needed washing
fairly badly by this stage of the meal.

Clean cups are now provided and the party moves into the 'sym-
posium' phase, which again features individually mixed drinks at
a variety of temperatures. The guests toast one another – politely
asking permission first – and the host encourages everyone to have
a drink. One guest, when asked why he is not drinking, points out
that he asked for wine and was not given any; rather than reacting to
this lamentable breach of hospitality by ordering a slave to come
immediately and serve the guest, the host seems to ignore the complaint. The reason is probably that the writer's chief goal was to
provide all the expressions hosts and guests would need at a dinner
party, not to tell a coherent story from beginning to end; orders to
slaves instructing them to serve guests have already been amply
illustrated, so the writer was unable to include another one here
without repetition. Nevertheless the modern reader may feel that at
the very least an illustration of an apology could have been provided
at this point.

Dessert food, here represented by sweet cheesecakes, is provided along with the drinks. At the end of this stage of the meal the party is over, so the guests ask for a lighted torch to enable them to see on the way home. In some versions of this scene the host provides not only a torch but also an escort for his guests on their way home; he may also offer to let them sleep at his house overnight. These guests, however, simply take their torch and depart, uttering the traditional polite expression of thanks for a good dinner: *bene nos accepisti* 'You have entertained us well.' As soon as they have left, the host directs the slaves to clear the dining room and put everything away.

9.4 ANOTHER DINNER PARTY

This version of the dinner scene (Colloquium Montepessulanum 16f–19b) is shorter and less detailed, but it includes a few points not seen in the previous passage. Some of the dishes arrive in the dining room needing to be carved or otherwise finished off before they are eaten ('do the stalks' must refer to some such procedure with a vegetable, perhaps the addition of sauce). Neither the host nor any of the guests could carve, since reclining diners had only one free hand, and therefore this type of work had to be done by the waiters; in fact the servants usually made sure that all food was cut into bite-sized pieces before being served, as without such preparation diners would have had a difficult time with it.

In sharp contrast to passage 9.2, which lists primarily vegetable dishes, this dinner consists primarily of meat. The dishes served include the uterus and udder of a sow, both of which were delicacies in antiquity (see the recipes in chapter 11.7); the uterus was said to be especially tasty if the sow had been forced to have a miscarriage before slaughter. Udders were eaten with fish paste, a salty and strong-tasting by-product of garum manufacture. Colostrum, now generally considered unfit for human consumption, is the milk produced in the first few days after the birth of a calf, lamb, or kid; it is thicker and sweeter than ordinary milk. Shad is a kind of fish.

Our friends have come! Mix wine for us. Let's recline. First give us beet greens or gourds. Add fish-sauce. Give us radishes and a knife. Put out fish-sauce made with vinegar, lettuces, and cucumbers. Bring out the pig's foot and paunch and sow's uterus. Give us bread made from fine wheat. Add oil to the salted fish. Skin the shad and put it on the table. Give us mustard, the neck meat, and the thigh bone. The fish has been roasted. Carve the venison, the wild boar, the chicken, and the hare. Do the stalks. Cut up the tender boiled meat. Give us roasted meat, and give us something to drink. Now we have all drunk. Bring on the turtledoves and the pheasant. Bring the udder and fish-paste. Pour the sauce. Let's eat! It is perfectly cooked. Give us roast suckling pig. It is sizzling hot. Carve it. Bring honey in a little cup. Also, bring a fattened goose seasoned with salt. Bring water to wash our hands. If you have got it, bring colostrum with honey, and halva. Cut the cake; let's take the pieces. We have been well entertained. Give the servants something to eat and drink, and give something to the cook, because he has served well. It is time to go.

9.5 A PRIVATE DINNER

Romans did not invite guests every evening. In this passage (Colloquium Montepessulanum 20a–c) a man comes home and eats a simple meal by himself. He is served by his wife, but she does not eat with him; she may have eaten already, as the hour is stated to be late.

It's now late; let's go home.

HE: Where's my wife?

SHE: Here I am.

HE: Have we got anything to eat?

SHE: We've got everything.

HE (*to slaves*): Set up the table, give me bread, cut the cheese, give me fruit.

SHE: Do you want any good olives?

HE: Just give me slices of meat and a plate of cheese . . .

CHAPTER 10

Bedtime

The Colloquia end with the end of the day: the main character returns home, if he has been out for the evening, and orders the slaves to prepare the house for the night.

10.1 THE AFTERMATH OF AN ORGY

Romans who had gone out to dinner did not always return in good condition. This passage (Colloquium Celtis 66a–68b) describes the heated reception that someone at home (probably a wife, but perhaps a male friend or relative) gives to a man very much the worse for wear. The public shame and humiliation attached to the man's behaviour are ruthlessly pointed out; unfortunately for the modern reader, who might like to know what type of drunken antics would lead to this kind of censure, we are not told exactly what the behaviour was. The drunk, who is not feeling well, does not even try to defend himself.

It is uncertain whether this passage is intended as a moral example, a warning to readers about what would happen if they overindulged, or whether the writer simply offered it as a useful set of expressions that one might need in such a situation.

> WIFE: Sir, is there anyone who acts like you and drinks as much as you do? What will the people who saw you in this condition say? That never before have you acted so greedily at a dinner party? Is this the way to behave when you are a respectable father, someone to whom others come for advice? It's impossible to act more shamefully or ignominiously than you did yesterday.
>
> HUSBAND: I certainly am very much ashamed.
>
> WIFE: What are other people saying behind your back? You have got yourself great infamy and blame through such

intemperance! Please never do anything like this again. Oh no, do you need to vomit now? I can't believe this!

HUSBAND: I don't know what to say; I'm so upset that I can't explain anything to anyone.

10.2 REBUKING THE SERVANTS

Drunken husbands were not the only people who might need to be chastised in the evening. If the slaves had done poorly during the day, a careful master would be sure to point this out before going to bed. In this passage (Colloquia Monacensia–Einsidlensia 12b–d) a master rebukes his slaves for being slow – evidently a common fault among slaves, for instructions to hurry up are found throughout the Colloquia – and confines them to quarters overnight as punishment. He also gets them to prepare his bed, and points out that it is their job to wake him early in the morning. An ancient bed had to be freshly prepared for each night because the mattress – essentially a large bag full of straw or a similar compressible substance – became hard in the course of the night as it was slept on; giving the bag a good shake redistributed the straw and fluffed it up, making it more comfortable to sleep on.

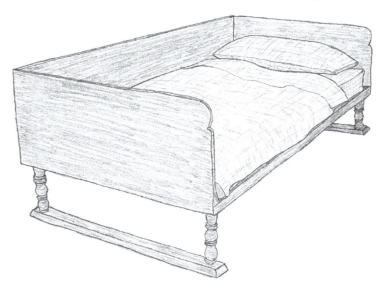

FIG. 54 A Roman bed, fluffed up and ready to be slept in (reconstruction at Xanten Archaeological Park, Germany)

MASTER: Get my bed ready, carefully.

SLAVES: We've done it.

MASTER: So why is the bed so hard?

SLAVES: We shook it out, and we softened up the pillow.

MASTER: Since you were slow to do your job, none of you may go out tonight. And be quiet – I'm going to punish anyone whose voice I hear. Go to bed, sleep, and wake me at cock-crow, so I can have an early start.

10.3 PREPARING FOR BED

Going to bed in a Roman house was not completely straightforward, as these passages (Colloquium Montepessulanum 20d–f and Colloquium Celtis 65, 69a–b) show.

HE: What time is it?

SHE: It's already the third hour of the night.

HE: Set out the chamber pot, the basin, and a jug of water. Call a boy to wash my feet – no, actually, call one of the women for that. Then remove the lamp. I want to sleep, so that I can wake up early in the morning.

*****

Put out the lamps and cover the fireplace carefully ... Boys, close the doors and the shutters. Put up the bars and set out the chamber pot. Go and get some rest.

The various flames used around the house for heat and light all needed to be either put out or secured so that they would not start a fire during the night. Yet one could not simply let them all go out, for lighting a fire was difficult in an age before matches: one fire, usually on the main hearth, had to be covered in such a way that it would burn gently throughout the night, without requiring any more fuel before morning.

Doors were closed and secured by means of heavy bars that completely blocked them on the inside; this was necessary to keep out intruders. The closing of shutters on windows kept out not only humans and animals but also cold air, since windows did not usually have glass (though in urban areas they often had metal bars).

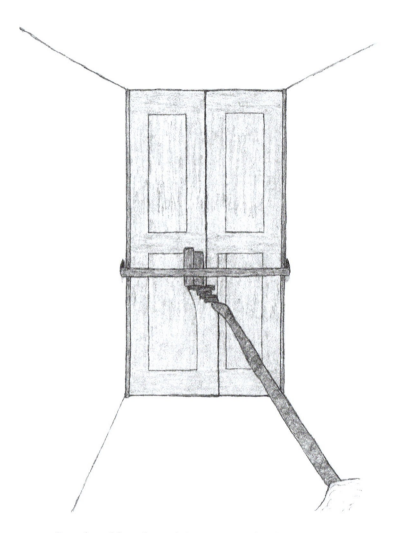

FIG. 55 Doors barred from the inside (reconstruction based on a plaster cast of first-century barred doors at Pompeii): one bar runs across both doors from wall to wall, while another braces them against a specially-constructed projection further down the passage. The left-hand door overlaps the right-hand one at the point where this second bar is set, making it impossible to force either half open independently, and two vertical pieces of wood brace the left-hand door against the horizontal bar.

FIG. 56 First-century clay chamber pot in Pompeii, Italy (inv. SAP 31699); partly restored

Moving around the house at night was difficult, since it was completely dark and the only way to get light was to make one's way to the covered fire, from which an oil lamp could be lighted; one could of course awaken a slave and ask him to light a lamp, but the process was time-consuming and best avoided. For this reason even people in houses with their own toilets used chamber pots at night and relied on slaves to empty them in the morning, clean them, and set them out again in the evening.

A jug of water and a basin for washing the next morning might also be put out at night, so that the master could wash in the morning without waiting for the servants to bring water. There was a disadvantage to this practice in cold weather, however: the only way to get warm water for washing was to have it heated in the morning. For this reason most of the morning scenes of the Colloquia depict characters asking for water to be brought in the morning, rather than using water that has been set out the night before.

The ancients often wore sandals or other open shoes, through which the wearer's feet quickly became covered with dust and dirt. (Although the most important Roman roads were paved with stone blocks, many roads were only dirt tracks.) As a result people often washed their feet either when they arrived home in the evening or before going to bed.

10.4 THE CONCLUSION

At the end of the text the writer sometimes appended a 'the end' statement, echoing the hope expressed at the start that the work would turn out fortunately. This one is from the Colloquium Harleianum (25e).

I have written felicitously about daily speech.

CHAPTER II

Passages Providing Additional Context for the Colloquia

The passages in this section are not from the Colloquia, but rather from other imperial-period texts that shed additional light on issues raised in the Colloquia and can to advantage be read along with them.

II.I PHILOGELOS

The work known as Philogelos ('laughter-lover') is a Greek joke book composed in the fourth century. It sheds light on many of the more absurd aspects of Roman society and the characters involved in that society. For more information and a translation of the entire joke book, see Baldwin (1983).

Joke 34

A learned fool went to visit a sick friend and asked him how he was. But when the friend did not answer, he grew angry and said, 'I hope to be sick myself, and then I'll not answer you!'

Joke 54

A learned fool, writing a letter from Athens to his father and being conceited at the education he had received there, added, 'I pray to come home and find you on trial for your life, so that I can show you what an orator I am.'

Joke 61

A learned fool of a primary-school teacher suddenly looked in the corner and shouted, 'Dionysios is misbehaving in the corner!' But one of the other children said that Dionysios was not there yet, to which the teacher responded, 'He will be misbehaving when he comes!'

Joke 70

A learned fool went to see a sick friend, but the man's wife said that he had already departed [i.e. died]. The man replied, 'So when he returns, tell him that I was here.'

Joke 91

A learned fool invited acquaintances to dinner, and they praised the pig's head he served and advised him to eat from it the next day as well. So he went to the butcher and said, 'Give me another head from the same pig, for the one we had yesterday was very successful.'

Joke 140

A joker seeing a stupid primary-school teacher teaching asked him why he did not teach the cithara. And when the teacher said, 'Because I do not know how', he said, 'So how do you teach letters when you do not know them either?'

Joke 150

When a joker was at the baths two people asked to borrow his strigil, one being a stranger and the other a known thief. The joker said, 'To you, on the one hand, I won't lend it because I don't know you; but to you on the other I won't lend it because I do know you.'

Joke 163

The people of Cyme, expecting an honoured foreign ally to visit them and wanting to honour him with clean water in the baths, but having only one pool, filled it with clean hot water and put a perforated grille down the middle in order to keep half the water clean for the awaited guest.

Joke 193

Someone came to see a grumpy man, and he responded, 'I'm not here!' When the visitor laughed and said, 'You're lying, for I hear your voice!' he said, 'Scum! if my slave had said it, you would have believed it: and don't I look to you more worthy of belief than he is?'

Joke 194

A grumpy man going down the stairs of his building slipped and fell. And when the house-master said, 'Who is out there?' he replied, 'I tripped up on my rent-payment. What is it to you?'

Joke 197

A stupid teacher, when asked, 'What was Priam's mother called?' and not knowing the answer, replied, 'We call her "madam" out of respect.'

Joke 220

A gluttonous teacher, seeing a loaf of bread hanging from the ceiling, said, 'Are you going to come down and recite your lesson, or do I have to go up and teach you?'

Joke 226

A gluttonous comic actor asked the person producing the play to give him lunch before he went onstage. And when he asked why he wanted to eat lunch first, the actor said, 'So that I shall not swear falsely when I say, "By Artemis, I for one have had an excellent lunch!"'

Joke 264

A joker on trial, seeing the judge dozing, shouted, 'I appeal!' And he said, 'To whom?' And the joker replied, 'To you – to wake up!'

11.2 GRAFFITI FROM POMPEII

Buried by a volcanic eruption in AD 79, the walls of the Roman city of Pompeii preserve many scratched and painted comments that would not have lasted long had they been exposed to normal weathering. Most are written in Latin, but a few use other languages. Many of these wall writings are not what we think of as graffiti, but rather the type of announcements that would today be printed on posters or billboards: notices of forthcoming gladiatorial shows, campaign advertisements for elections, advertisements for businesses, etc. Some, however, are simply private scribbles – not always rude, but often so. The examples below are selected as complements to the insults in passage 6.3. For more information on Pompeii and translations of further graffiti and inscriptions, see Cooley and Cooley (2014) and Beard (2008).

CIL IV. 1813

Woe to you!

CIL IV. 1864

Samius to Cornelius: hang yourself!

CIL IV. 2082

May you be crucified!

CIL IV. 2409a

Stronnius knows nothing.

CIL IV. 4764

Perarius, you are a thief.

CIL IV. 6864

Best and greatest Jupiter, all-powerful lord! Acratus is a useless slave.

CIL IV. 8322k

Somene is useless.

11.3 VINDOLANDA TABLETS

From Vindolanda in northern Britain come a set of wooden tablets containing the Latin correspondence of Roman soldiers and their families in the late first and early second centuries. The frequent use of 'brother' and 'sister' in these documents should not be taken literally: during the Roman empire these words were used to friends as terms of endearment much more often than to actual relatives. For more information on the Vindolanda tablets, and for texts and translations of more letters, see Bowman (2003) and the Vindolanda web site (http://vindolanda.csad.ox.ac.uk).

In tablet 291 a date (11th September in our terms) is reckoned in Roman fashion, by counting backward from a festival: the Ides was a festival that could fall on the 13th or 15th of a month. In September it fell on the 13th, and Romans counted inclusively, so for them the 11th was the third day before the 13th. As in Colloquium passage 7.2, no time is specified.

In tablet 343 two dates are given by festivals: the Kalends was always the first day of the month, and the Ides fell on the 13th in January.

T. Vindol. 11.291

Claudia Severa to her Lepidina, greetings.

I warmly ask you, sister, to make sure you come to us on the day of celebration of my birthday, on the third day before the Ides of September. You will make the day more enjoyable for me by your presence! Greet your husband Cerialis; my husband Aelius and my little son greet you. I shall expect you, sister. Farewell, sister, my dearest soul (so may I be well), and hail.

T. Vindol. 11.343

Octavius to his brother Candidus, greetings.

With regard to the hundred pounds of sinew from Marinus, I shall sort out payment; since you wrote about this issue he has not even mentioned it to me. Several times I wrote to you that I bought ears of grain, nearly five thousand *modii*, on account of which I need money. If you do not send me some, at least five hundred denarii, what will happen is that I shall lose my deposit, about three hundred denarii, and shall be embarrassed. So please, as soon as you can, send me some!

The hides which you tell me are at Cataractonium, tell the people there to give them to me, and the cart about which you write; and tell me what is with the cart. I would have gone there to get them before now, except that I did not care to wear out the draft animals while the roads are bad. Talk to Tertius about the 8½ denarii that he received from Fatalis; he has not credited them to me.

Know that I have finished 170 hides and have 119 *modii* of threshed grain. Make sure to send me money so that I can have ears of grain for threshing; I have already completely finished threshing everything I had. A messmate of our friend Frontius was here; he wanted me to assign hides to him and was going to pay cash for them. I said that I would give him the hides by the Kalends of March. On the Ides of January he agreed that he would come, but he did not show up, and he did not care to receive them, since he had hides already. If he had given the money, I would have given him the hides. I hear that Frontinius Iulius is asking a high price for the leather goods that he bought here for five denarii each.

Greet Spectatus and Firmus. I have received letters from Gleuco. Farewell.

II.4 OXYRHYNCHUS PAPYRI

Thousands of papyrus fragments survive from the town of Oxyrhynchus in Egypt, which flourished during the Roman period; these offer a glimpse into the lives of ordinary people, from their tax returns and loan contracts to the poetry they read and the letters they wrote to friends and family. Most of the papyri (including all the examples given below) are in Greek, but a few use Latin or Egyptian. For further information and more examples see Parsons (2007) and the Oxyrhynchus papyri web site (www.papyrology.ox.ac.uk/POxy/).

The letter in *P.Oxy.* 1.119, from a boy to his father, was written in the second or third century and illustrates one reason why a parent might have taken a child with him on business when that child should have been in school. The one in *SB* III.6262, written in the third century by a would-be student to his father, reveals a different kind of family tension; here the teacher's reluctance to begin training the writer probably stems from the fact that the father was supposed to make or arrange payment when he arrived. A more attentive parent appears in *P.Oxy.* VI.930, the end of a letter from a second- or third-century mother to her son (the first part of the letter is lost).

Invitations are also common in the Oxyrhynchus papyri; when involving dinner these often specify a time of the ninth hour, which would have been around 3 p.m. (for Roman hours see the explanation of Colloquium passage 3.3). The example in *P.Oxy.* VI.926 comes from the third century.

P.Oxy. I.119

Theon to his father Theon, greetings.

You did well when you didn't take me with you to the city! If you don't take me with you to Alexandria I shall not write you any letters nor speak to you nor say goodbye to you, and if you go to Alexandria without me I shall absolutely not take your hand or ever greet you again. If you do not want to take me that is what will happen. And my mother said to Archelaos that 'He is upsetting me, take him away!' You did well to send me big presents, a hill of beans. They put us off the track on the day when you sailed, the 12th. Please, send for me! If you do not send for me I shall absolutely not eat and not drink. So there! I pray that you be well.

P.Oxy. VI.926

Heratheon invites you to dinner at his house on the occasion of his coming-of-age ceremony, tomorrow, that is the 5th, from the ninth hour.

P.Oxy. VI.930

Do not hesitate to write to me about whatever you may need. Here I was sorry to hear from the daughter of our teacher Diogenes that he has sailed away. For I was not worried about him, knowing that he was going to look after you as well as he could. And I took care to send a letter and ask about your health and find out what you are reading. And he said it was the sixth book of the *Iliad*, and he told me a lot about your paedagogue. So, son, you and your paedagogue should take care to find yourself a suitable teacher. Your sisters send you many greetings, as do the children of Theonis (may the evil eye stay away from them), and all of us greet you by name. Give my greetings to your esteemed paedagogue Eros.

SB III.6262

To my lord father Arion, Thonis sends greetings.

Before all I prostrate myself every day on your behalf before the ancestral gods here where I am a guest, and pray that I may get you back again entirely healthy, along with all our people. Look, I am now writing to you for the fifth time, and you have not written to me, except just once, not even about your health, and you have not come to me. Having promised 'I'm coming,' you did not come so that you could find out whether the teacher is paying attention to me or not. So he too inquires almost every day about you, 'Isn't he coming yet?' And so I say one thing, 'Yes.' So make haste to come quickly to me, so that he will teach me, as he is eager to do. If you had come up with me, I would have been taught long ago. But when you come, remember what I have often written to you. So come quickly to us, before he goes away upriver. I send many greetings to all our people by name, along with our friends, and I also greet my teachers. Farewell, my lord father, and I pray that you may have good fortune for many years, along with my brothers (may the evil eye stay away from them). P.S.: Remember our pigeons!

II.5 THE POEMS OF MARTIAL

The Roman poet Martial, who lived in the first century AD, wrote hundreds of short Latin poems known as 'epigrams'. Some of these are self-explanatory, while others have titles that provide the key to their meaning. For the complete text and translation of the epigrams, see Shackleton Bailey (1993).

Epigram 4.8 describes the typical activities of different hours in a Roman day, from sunrise (the first hour) to sunset (the twelfth hour). Epigrams 6.19 and 8.17 depict the lawyer–client relationship rather differently from the rose-tinted view offered in the Colloquia: in 6.19 a client complains about his lawyer, and in 8.17 a lawyer complains about his client. In epigram 7.17 Martial reveals that although he did not intend to copy out himself the presentation copy of his poetry for the dedicatee, he expected to go over it himself and correct the mistakes made by the copyist; note the assumption that there would be mistakes.

The poems from book 14 are intended to be inscribed on various objects, often gifts to friends. The titles indicate the objects on which each poem was intended to be written. In 14.51 the object is a pair of strigils, the scrapers used to remove sweat and dirt after exercise and after bathing in a Roman bath; note the reference to the towels, which implies that a towel used to dry oneself after bathing became dirty less quickly if the bather first removed the residue of dirty bath water with a strigil. Evidently Martial envisioned the strigils being used after bathing, as in passages 8.2, 8.3, and 8.4. In the others, the object is a book in the parchment codex format, which in Martial's time was just starting to be used in Rome; it would take several more centuries before the codex supplanted the papyrus roll in Egypt. Because a codex used both sides of the writing material and did not have a hole in the middle the way a roll did, the codex allowed a long text to be compressed into a much smaller space than had previously been possible, and it is this smallness that Martial finds particularly noteworthy. The codex of Livy mentioned in epigram 14.190, however, may be a summary rather than the complete work.

Epigram 4.8

The first and second hours of the day exhaust people who are obliged to greet their patrons in the morning, and the third hour keeps loud-mouthed lawyers busy. Public business extends through the end of the fifth, the sixth and seventh offer rest for those who are tired, the eighth suffices for well-oiled exercises, and the end of the ninth commands us to land on the couches for dinner. The hour for my little books of poetry, Euphemus, is the tenth, when you take care to provide well-appointed, ambrosial feasts and kind Caesar, relaxing with heavenly nectar, holds moderate cups in his mighty hand. Then let the jokes come in: our muse is too timid for the morning hours.

Epigram 6.19

My lawsuit is not about assault and battery, or murder, or poisoning: it is about three goats, which I claim are absent because of theft by a neighbour. The judge asks for this to be proved to him: you declaim about Carrhae and the Mithridatic war and the perjuries of Carthaginian rage and Sullas and Mariuses and Muciuses, using a loud voice and waving your whole arm. Now, Postumus, talk about my three goats.

Epigram 7.17

O library of a charming country villa, from which the reader can see the neighbouring city: if there happens to be any space for lascivious poetry among the more serious works, you are permitted to place in a niche, even the lowest one, these seven little books that we have sent to you. They have been annotated by the pen of their author: these corrections make the books valuable. But may you, library of Julius Martialis, take good care of this pledge of my heart, enchanted by the little gift that will cause you to be known to the whole world through the recitation of this poem.

Epigram 8.17

Sextus, you promised me two thousand sesterces, and I pleaded your case. How is it that you then sent me one thousand? You say, 'You did not explain anything, and you lost the case.' You owe me more for that, Sextus, because it was embarrassing.

Epigram 14.51

Strigils

These come from Pergamum. Scrape yourself with the curved iron, and your towels will not be worn out by such frequent washing.

Epigram 14.184

Homer in parchment notebooks
The *Iliad* and *Odyssey* both lie hidden here, stored in many skins.

Epigram 14.186

Virgil on parchment

How little parchment it takes to hold great Virgil! The first page bears a picture of the author.

Epigram 14.190

Livy on parchment

Enormous Livy, for whose complete work my library does not have space, is here compressed into a few skins.

11.6 SENECA, LETTER 56.1–2

The first-century philosopher Seneca the Younger (not to be confused with the rhetorician Seneca the Elder) wrote a set of elegant Latin letters about Stoic philosophy. In this passage he points out the disadvantages of living over the baths – though these are mitigated in his case by his Stoic ability to ignore the noise.

Look how many different kinds of noise shout at me from all sides! I live right over a private bath. Picture for yourself all the kinds of sounds that can make one hate one's ears: when too-strong men exercise and whirl their arms around while lifting weights, when they either strain away or pretend to strain, I hear their groans, panting, and gasps every time they exhale; when the person below me is inert and content with an ordinary rub-down, I hear the slap of the hand coming down on his shoulder – different sounds according to whether the hand lands flat or cupped. If a score-keeper comes along and begins to count the score for the ball games, all is lost. Now add the arrest of thieves and troublemakers and the people who enjoy hearing their own voices in the baths. And now add the people who jump into the pool with a huge splash. In addition to those people, whose voices are, if nothing else, at least normal, think about the shrill, strident voice of the hair-plucker, constantly calling out to advertise himself and never shutting up except when he makes other people yell instead by plucking their armpits. And then there are the various calls of the people hawking cakes, sausages, pastries, and all types of food, each trying to sell his wares by his own distinctive cries.

11.7 APICIUS' COOKBOOK

The Latin recipe book bearing the name of Apicius may date to the fourth century. It is arranged by dishes, so each section contains several different recipes for preparing the same general dish. Three sections are included here, the first with six different recipes and the second and third with two recipes each; these recipes are fairly typical in the lack of detailed instructions or specific quantities of ingredients. For more information on Apicius and a complete translation of the cookbook, see Grocock and Grainger (2006).

Section 7.1

How to prepare a uterus, uterus of a young sow, pork-rind, pig's snout, pig's tail, and pig's trotter
1 Uterus or uterus of a young sow: serve with silphium-juice from Cyrenaica or Parthia mixed with vinegar and fish-sauce.
2 For a uterus or uterus of a young sow: serve with pepper, celery seed, dry mint, silphium root, honey, vinegar, and fish-sauce.
3 Uterus and uterus of a young sow: serve with pepper, fish-sauce, and silphium-juice from Parthia.
4 Uterus and uterus of a young sow: serve with pepper, fish-sauce, and a little spiced wine.
5 Pork-rind, pig's snout, pig's tail, and pig's trotter: serve with pepper, fish-sauce, and silphium juice.
6 How to grill a uterus: roll it in bran, then put it in brine and cook it like that.

Section 7.2

Udder
1 Boil the udder thoroughly, tie it up with reeds, sprinkle it with salt, and put it in the oven or on the grill. Cook it lightly. Grind pepper, lovage, and fish-sauce, moisten them with pure wine and with raisin-wine, bind the mixture with starch, and spread it on the udder.
2 Stuffed udder: grind pepper, caraway seed, and a salted sea-urchin; (put them inside and) sew up the udder, and cook it like that. This dish is eaten with fish-paste and mustard.

Section 7.7

Stomach

1   Pig's stomach: empty it completely, wash it with salt and vinegar, then wash it with water. Fill it with the following stuffing. Mix ground and pounded pork with three brains from which the sinews have been removed, and raw eggs. Add pine nuts and whole peppercorns, and mix it with the following sauce. Grind pepper, lovage, silphium, aniseed, ginger, a little rue, best-quality fish-sauce, and a little oil. Fill the stomach, leaving space so that it does not explode during cooking. Tie off both openings and immerse it in a pot of boiling water; then take it out and prick it with a sharp implement, so that it does not burst. When it is half cooked, take it out and hang it in smoke to give it a good colour. Boil it again thoroughly, so that it is fully cooked, this time with fish-sauce, pure wine, and a little oil. Open it with a knife and serve with fish-sauce and lovage.

2   How to grill a stomach: roll it in bran, then put it in brine and cook it like that.

11.8   THE EDICT OF DIOCLETIAN

In the third century the Roman empire experienced severe inflation, with damaging consequences for the people and the government. In an effort to curtail rising prices, the emperor Diocletian issued an edict on maximum prices in AD 301. This document lists a vast range of goods and services and the maximum legal price that could be charged for each; as a means of price control it may not have been entirely effective, but as a way of recording for posterity what was traded at that period and the relative values of different commodities, it is unequalled. The edict was produced in both Greek and Latin and set up as inscriptions all over the empire; although no copies survive intact, much of the text can be reconstructed by putting together the fragments of different copies that remain. The extracts reproduced here are the end of the introduction and section 7 of the price list.

Prices are expressed using the denarius, which after the third century was no longer issued as a coin but which remained in common use as a unit for expressing value throughout the empire. The extent of the price rise that Diocletian was prepared to accept can be judged from the fact that in the early empire one denarius represented a day's wage for an unskilled worker. For a full translation of the Edict see Graser (1940).

> Justly and rightly moved by all the things explained above, now, when mankind itself seems to pray for help, we have determined it necessary to establish not the prices of items for sale (for doing that did not seem just, when many provinces from time to time rejoice in the blessing of hoped-for low prices and something like the privilege of affluence), but an upper limit, so that, when the violence of high prices appears (may the gods prevent such a disaster!), avarice, which previously could not be restrained, as if it were running free in extensive fields, now might be contained by the limits of our statute or the boundaries of a restricting law. It is our pleasure, therefore, that the prices in the attached summary be observed in our whole empire, in such a way that everyone understands that the freedom to exceed them is denied him, while at the same time in those places where an abundance can be observed there is no impediment to the blessing of low prices, a blessing particularly provided for when avarice is decidedly restrained.
>
> Moreover among merchants who customarily visit ports and foreign provinces, this universal decree should act as a restraint so that, since they themselves know that they cannot exceed the decreed maximums in a time of high prices, at the time of sale a reckoning be made of the cost of transportation and the whole business, by which it should be clear that we have rightly determined that those who transport goods should nowhere sell them for higher prices than those we have established.
>
> Because it is agreed that also in the time of our ancestors it was the custom in making laws to restrain insolence by a prescribed penalty (because it is very rare for a benefit to humanity to be voluntarily accepted, and fear is found to be the best enforcer of duty), it is our pleasure that if anyone contravenes the letter of this law, he shall die for his audacity. And let no-one think the law harsh, since there is at hand a way of avoiding danger, by observing restraint. But the same penalty will apply also to the buyer who conspires with the greed of the seller against the law. Nor shall anyone be immune to this penalty who, although having the

necessities of life and business, thinks that after this decree he should withdraw them from the market; since the penalty of introducing poverty should be even more severe than that of afflicting the poor against the law.

Therefore we urge our devoted populace to observe with willing obedience and due respect a law designed for the public good, especially since in a law of this type provision is made not for individual states, peoples, or provinces, but for the whole world, toward whose ruin only a very few people would rampage, people whose avarice could be lessened or satisfied neither by time nor by the riches for which they appeared to strive.

The prices that no-one is allowed to exceed in selling individual items are listed here below: . . .

About the Wages of Workers

For a farm labourer who is also given food	per day	25 den.
For a stonemason who is also given food	per day	50 den.
For a cabinet maker, as above	per day	50 den.
For a carpenter, as above	per day	50 den.
For a lime burner, as above	per day	50 den.
For a marble worker, as above	per day	60 den.
For a mosaic setter doing pictures, as above	per day	60 den.
For a mosaic setter doing coarse work, as above	per day	50 den.
For a wall painter, as above	per day	75 den.
For a figure painter, as above	per day	150 den.
For a wagon maker, as above	per day	50 den.
For a blacksmith, as above	per day	50 den.
For a baker, as above	per day	50 den.
For a ship-builder of seagoing vessels, as above	per day	60 den.
For a ship-builder of river boats, as above	per day	50 den.
The daily wage for someone who makes bricks for firing, for every four two-foot bricks, when he also prepares the clay, and when he is also given food		2 den.

Also the daily wage for someone who makes unbaked bricks, for every eight bricks, when he also prepares the clay, and when he is also given food		2 den.
For the driver of a camel, donkey, or hinny, when he is also given food	per day	25 den.
For a shepherd who is also given food	per day	25 den.
For a mule-driver who is also given food	per day	25 den.
For a veterinarian, for the trimming and fitting of hoofs	per animal	6 den.
for bleeding and purging the head	per animal	20 den.
For a barber	per person	2 den.
For a sheep-shearer who is also given food	per animal	2 den.

About bronze-working

For a copper smith, for work in brass	per pound	8 den.
for work in copper	per pound	6 den.
for small vessels of various types	per pound	6 den.
for figurines or statues	per pound	4 den.
for bronze inlay	per pound	6 den.
Daily wage for a model-maker who is also given food		75 den.
For other kinds of plaster-workers who are also given food	per day	50 den.
For a water carrier who works all day and is also given food	per day	25 den.
For a sewer cleaner who works all day and is also given food	per day	25 den.
For a sharpener/polisher, for a used sword		25 den.
for a used helmet		25 den.
for an axe		6 den.
for a double-bladed axe		8 den.
for the scabbard of a sword		100 den.
For a parchment maker, for a one-foot-square quaternion of white or yellow parchment		40 den.

For a book scribe, for best-quality writing	per 100 lines	25 den.
for second-quality writing	per 100 lines	20 denarii
For a notary, for writing a petition or legal documents	per 100 lines	10 denarii
For a tailor, for cutting out and finishing, for a cloak of first quality		60 den.
for a cloak of second quality		40 den.
for a large hood		25 den.
for a small hood		20 den.
for trousers		20 den.
for socks		4 den.
For a stitcher, for folding and sewing a light garment		6 den.
For the same, for a silk neck-band and sewing it on		50 den.
For the same, for a partly silk neck-band and sewing it on		30 den.
for sewing a coarser garment		4 den.
A horse blanket made of felt, black or white, weighing 3 pounds		100 den.
A blanket of first quality, embroidered, of the weight written above		250 den.
For a dyer, for a woman's ordinary tunic, if new		16 den.
if used		10 den.
for a man's shirt, if new		10 den.
if used		6 den.
for a child's garment, if new		6 den.
if used		2 den.
for a short mantle, if new		16 den.
if used		6 den.
for a coverlet, if new		24 den.
if used		10 den.
For a gymnastics trainer, per pupil	per month	50 den.
For a paedagogue, per child	per month	50 den.
For a primary school teacher, per child	per month	50 den.
For a mathematics teacher, per child	per month	75 den.
For a shorthand teacher, per child	per month	75 den.
For a scribe-trainer, per pupil	per month	50 den.

For a teacher of Greek or Latin grammar/literature and for a geometry teacher, per pupil	per month	200 den.
For a teacher of oratory or rhetoric, per pupil	per month	250 den.
For a lawyer, for presenting a case		250 den.
for pleading a case		1000 den.
For a teacher of architecture, per child	per month	100 den.
For a clothes-watcher, per person bathing		2 den.
For the keeper of a private bath, per person bathing		2 den.

Further Information about the Colloquia

12.1 THE COLLOQUIA

The Colloquia are a set of ancient easy readers for language students. They were originally composed bilingually, in Greek and Latin, and were used both by Latin speakers learning Greek and by Greek speakers learning Latin. Most Colloquia are amalgams of two parts that were originally separate: the first describes the day of a schoolboy from dawn until lunchtime or shortly afterwards, and the second contains scenes that an adult might engage in during the day and evening.

The first of these two portions, known as the schoolbook, is demonstrably related in all the different Colloquia versions: there was once a single schoolbook from which all the extant versions are descended. That original version was composed in the Western part of the Roman world, probably in Rome, to help Latin-speaking children learn Greek. It was in use by the first century AD and may be much older than that. In the first or second century the schoolbook was borrowed by Greek speakers in the Eastern empire, who adapted it as a tool for learning Latin. As it was bilingual to begin with, the changes needed were minimal.

The second part of the Colloquia, known as the phrasebook, comes from the Eastern empire and was composed to help Greek speakers learn Latin. The different versions of the phrasebook are certainly related to some extent, but the relationship is much less close than that of the different schoolbook versions, and it is not clear that all the extant versions go back to one original: different phrasebooks may have been composed separately. The phrasebooks are later in origin than the schoolbook, dating probably to the second century AD. Their original form was probably that of a modern phrasebook, without any connected story line, but in most versions the collections of phrases on each topic were later transformed into coherent scenes.

The Colloquia as we have them are the product of a long period of adaptation and evolution. Successive teachers rewrote various scenes to make them more useful for the particular students by whom they were used, and thus the single original text split into different versions. Those different versions then gradually diverged more and more from one another. Most of the actual wording of the texts we have probably comes from the second and third centuries, but some is earlier and some comes from the fourth century or even later. Some specific passages can be identified from their content or language as coming from a particular century, but most cannot be dated with precision.

For further information see Dickey (2012–15: 1.3–56).

12.2 THE HERMENEUMATA PSEUDODOSITHEANA

The ancient Colloquia found in this book are not the only Colloquia that exist; the genre was popular not only in antiquity but also in the middle ages, Renaissance, and later. To distinguish them from later Colloquia, the ancient Colloquia are usually called the Colloquia of the Hermeneumata Pseudodositheana, because they are part of a vast conglomerate of ancient language-learning materials known as the Hermeneumata Pseudodositheana. The Hermeneumata Pseudodositheana consist primarily of Greek–Latin glossaries, some alphabetically arranged and some classified by topic (i.e. with one section containing words for gods, another words for objects made of silver, another words for animals, etc.). They also contain some originally monolingual texts that were adapted for language learners by adding a translation; these include selections from Aesop's fables and Hyginus' mythography. Such texts clearly have their origins outside the Hermeneumata tradition, and most of them are also well attested in their original monolingual forms. But the Colloquia are different from these other texts, since they were written specifically as language-learning tools and exist only in a bilingual format.

The title 'Hermeneumata', which has become established in English, is a borrowing of the Greek word Ἑρμηνεύματα that appears as the title of some Hermeneumata versions; the Latin equivalent is *Interpretamenta*, and the meaning is 'bilingual translations'. Several of the manuscripts containing Hermeneumata also contain the grammatical treatise bearing the name of Dositheus. Although this is manifestly a grammar of Latin, it has a partial Greek translation (the grammar was originally composed to help Greek speakers learn

Latin), and therefore it resembles the other Hermeneumata materials in being bilingual and in being potentially usable to learn either language. (Of course, using a grammar of Latin to learn Greek is not a good idea, but that did not prevent people from trying to use Dositheus' work in this fashion.) Modern scholars first encountered the Hermeneumata in the manuscripts that also include the grammar, and the initial assumption was that the whole body of language-learning material – Dositheus' grammar and the glossaries, texts, and Colloquia now known as the Hermeneumata – had a common origin. Since only the grammar had an author's name attached, early scholars coined the name 'Hermeneumata Dositheana' to refer to the material other than the grammar. Further study revealed that Dositheus' grammar is not closely connected to the Hermeneumata (most Hermeneumata manuscripts do not include it) and seems to have been composed considerably later. This led to the renaming of the collection as the 'Hermeneumata Pseudo-dositheana'.

The Hermeneumata, like the Colloquia, are found in many different versions, and broadly speaking each Colloquium version goes with a particular Hermeneumata version. Clearly the Colloquia were part of the Hermeneumata for a very long time and underwent much of their evolution and development in the context of the Hermeneumata. Nevertheless their origins appear to be separate from those of the Hermeneumata, which originally consisted only of a preface and glossaries. The Colloquia, like the other texts in the Hermeneumata, appear to have been added later to provide learners with reading material.

The Hermeneumata, like the schoolbook portion of the Colloquia, appear to come originally from the West and to have been designed for Latin speakers learning Greek. They were borrowed by Greek speakers wanting to learn Latin, who expanded and adapted the glossaries by adding words that were more useful to inhabitants of the Eastern empire than to those of the West. It seems to be these Greek speakers who attached the Colloquia to the Hermeneumata.

For further information see Dickey (2012–15: 1.16–44) and Dionisotti (1982), and for texts of most of the Hermeneumata see Goetz (1892) and Flammini (2004).

12.3 LANGUAGE STUDY IN ANTIQUITY: WHO AND WHY?

The Hermeneumata Pseudodositheana can best be understood in the context of the learning environment that produced them. In the ancient world multilingualism was common but usually did not result from systematic language teaching, since the mobility of trade, war, and the sale of slaves captured in war meant that children often grew up in environments where multiple languages were spoken and acquired them without conscious study. Such language acquisition leaves no traces for us to observe, though the multilingualism that resulted from it can often be documented and evaluated with fascinating results.

Sometimes, however, people wanted to learn a language that they were not going to acquire without conscious study; even if this type of language learning accounted for only a minority of the multilingualism in the Roman empire as a whole, it was significant in scope, to judge from the number of ancient documents relating to it that have been preserved. And it is clearly to this context that the Hermeneumata belong.

Large-scale language study seems to have been originally a Roman phenomenon. The classical Greeks were usually uninterested in language learning, but elite Roman society embraced the study of Greek from an early period, since the early Romans had a great respect for Greek culture and especially for Greek literature. Although some of the masterpieces of Greek literature could be read in Latin translation, the translations were widely recognised as being no substitute for the originals, and knowledge of the Greek language was considered an essential part of upper-class education. Parents made great efforts to ensure that their children learned Greek at an early age, by buying Greek-speaking slaves to raise the children and/or by having them taught Greek at school. In the early first century B C Cicero and Atticus studied Greek language and literature at school together and found the impact of that experience so great that in later life they tended to use Greek when discussing with each other the type of literary criticism they had done at school. The more advanced training of a Roman upper-class boy often included a lengthy trip to Athens to finish his studies in a fully Greek-speaking environment.

As the republic turned into the empire and Rome solidified her control of the Greek-speaking world, the position of Greek in Rome did not change. Greek language and literature retained its superior position despite Roman political dominance, and Roman children continued to study Greek throughout the imperial period and into late antiquity. This level of continuity means that a schoolbook designed to help such children learn Greek would have been useful for many centuries.

The growth of the empire led to an enormous expansion of the geographical spread of Latin. When the Romans conquered peoples in the West who spoke something other than Latin, those peoples usually ended up learning Latin and, eventually, losing their original languages entirely. That is why languages like French, Spanish, and Italian are descended from Latin rather than from the languages spoken in France, Spain, and Italy before the Roman conquest. We do not know whether this language shift involved any systematic study of Latin as a foreign language: no evidence of such study is preserved, but given the generally poor survival of school materials from these areas, systematic study could have been widespread without leaving any evidence for us to find. But even if it existed, systematic study of Latin as a foreign language would have been short-lived in regions such as Gaul, ceasing once Latin became the native language of the populations concerned.

The Romans also brought with them the idea that an educated citizen should learn Greek. The tendency to engage in systematic study of Greek thus often spread with Romanisation, though people in some parts of the Western empire had spoken Greek long before Romanisation (Marseilles in southern France, for example, was originally a Greek colony). There is evidence for the use of the Colloquia as a Greek-learning tool not only in Rome, but also in the Western provinces, where members of the elite were as keen to give their children a good education as were their counterparts in Rome.

The situation in the East was very different from that in the West. The conquests of Alexander the Great had established Greek as the language of literature, culture, and administration throughout enormous areas of the Eastern Mediterranean, and the Roman conquest did not fundamentally alter that situation. When the Romans conquered regions that already had fully developed government structures available to be exploited, their policy was generally to leave those structures intact, use them, and superimpose on top of them a relatively small number of high-ranking officials sent from Rome; therefore the Greek-speaking bureaucracies of the Eastern Mediterranean continued to function after the Roman conquest.

(Most of these were later reorganised as part of sweeping reforms in the late empire, and it is sometimes claimed that one effect of those reforms was increased use of Latin in the administration of Eastern provinces, but the evidence is by no means conclusive, and it is clear that Greek remained the primary language of the Eastern bureaucracies throughout the empire.) Although the local native languages of the East often died out like those of the West, their speakers seem largely to have shifted to Greek rather than to Latin. But the power of the Romans meant that knowledge of Latin could be advantageous in the East, and this advantage, when combined with the fact that the population did not become native Latin speakers, created a long-term demand for systematic Latin study.

The reasons for that demand were very different from those motivating the study of Greek in the West. The social and cultural cachet attached to Greek in the West was not immediately replicated for Latin in the East, since at the time of the Roman conquest Greek speakers fully agreed with the Romans about the superiority of Greek literature and culture. After all, by the time the Romans arrived the Greek-speaking elite had a long-established educational system of their own and a set of intellectual priorities focussed exclusively on their own language and literature.

But as Greek speakers were assimilated into the Roman world that attitude gradually changed, particularly outside Greece proper. People who did not consider themselves ethnically Greek, whose ancestors had learned Greek as a foreign language, were often happy to learn another language if they had a good reason to do so, while at the same time not wanting to bother without a good reason. Although many people never found themselves in a position where Latin would be useful, as time went on increasing numbers of Greek speakers decided that they needed some Latin. Such need did not arise primarily from travel to Latin-speaking regions; indeed it is striking how rarely travel vocabulary is found in the ancient language-learning materials (the Colloquia, for example, never mention sea voyages or other long-distance travel, nor do they cover overnight accommodation, asking directions in an unfamiliar city, or other travel-specific information). No doubt travellers to the West would have found Latin useful, but we have no evidence that this fact led them to embark on study of the language before leaving home. Instead, the motivation for Latin-learning in the East seems to have come chiefly from the need to use Latin closer to home, dealing with Latin speakers and contexts in which Latin was normally used.

Latin speakers were, of course, fairly common in the East, particularly in the larger population centres. Most Latin speakers also spoke Greek, but as they were often people with money and status there would have been advantages to being able to communicate with them in their own language. In addition to this general situation, there were two more specific groups of Easterners who stood to benefit from knowing Latin because of interactions with particularly Latin-oriented contexts: those dealing with the army and those practising law.

The army was not by any means exclusively Latin-speaking; in fact there is good evidence that in the East many army units were predominantly Greek-speaking. Nevertheless it had a Latin-speaking chain of command, and most units contained a significant number of Latin speakers. As army units were moved around in response to military needs, a primarily Latin-speaking unit might find itself in a Greek-speaking region, or vice versa. Greek speakers who joined the army therefore often learned Latin; some scholars believe that the army put on special language classes for these recruits, but the evidence is not conclusive.

The Roman army also had an effect on the surrounding population. As soon as a unit moved into an area it became one of the main markets for local produce, and when a permanent army base was established it provided a tremendous boost to the local economy. Most army purchasers were capable of negotiating in Greek, but an ability to speak Latin would no doubt have been an asset in the competition among farmers, fishermen, etc. to sell to the troops. For this reason some of the ancient language-learning materials focus on vocabulary that would be needed in trying to deal with the Roman army; such a focus is not, however, common in the Colloquia, which show more influence from the other strand of the Eastern Latin-learning tradition.

That other strand was the study of Roman law, since in theory, at least, Roman law was practised exclusively in Latin. This theory was not always followed in practice; we have numerous legal documents in Greek, and transcripts of court cases show that although they were opened and closed in Latin, the actual arguments were often conducted in Greek. In the late empire, when enormous codifications of Roman law were produced in Latin, they were often accompanied by notes and glosses in Greek. So it would not have been impossible to practise law in the East without knowing Latin, but nevertheless knowledge of Latin was a great advantage. And since law was a highly competitive career, law students often wanted to learn Latin.

The principle that knowledge of Greek carried social cachet in the West but knowledge of Latin did not carry equivalent social cachet in the East lasted until the fifth century. After the Germanic incursions and the fall of the Western empire, the two halves of the former Roman empire were effectively divided from one another, greatly reducing the practical value to inhabitants of either half of learning the language of the other. In the West, moreover, the education system underwent some changes; these used to be regarded as a collapse resulting in the steep decline of literacy and all types of knowledge, but in recent years this drastic view has been challenged. It may be unfair to say that the entire classical education system disappeared at the end of antiquity, but it is clear that knowledge of Greek did largely disappear from the West; whether or not it still carried social prestige, there were no longer many people who could claim that prestige.

In the East, of course, matters were different, for there was a continuity of government and of the education system. Nevertheless the Byzantines were not wholly unaffected by the fall of the Western empire; in particular the role of Latin changed dramatically when the Eastern empire became effectively the entire empire. Knowledge of Latin ceased to be practically useful except for specialists in Roman law, who in the sixth century were still using and indeed even creating Latin legal codifications. But in that century, just as its practical utility disappeared, Latin finally developed significant social prestige in the East. It became fashionable to use Latin words and phrases, even if many of the people using these phrases were not sure exactly what they meant, and indeed some such phrases became fossilised in the rituals of the Byzantine court and persisted through the intervening centuries, when no-one understood them at all.

For further information see Adams (2003, on bilingualism between Latin and other languages in both East and West), Mullen (2013) and Mullen and James (2012, both on multilingualism in antiquity), Rochette (1997, on the role of Latin in the East; 1998, extensive bibliographic survey; 2008, on the use of the Hermeneumata), and Dickey (2012–15: especially 1.4–15).

12.4 LANGUAGE STUDY IN ANTIQUITY: HOW?

Latin speakers learning Greek had to begin with the alphabet, just like modern learners of Greek. Greek speakers learning Latin often did the same thing, but sometimes they did not bother with the alphabet and learned Latin in transliteration. Such learners must have been aiming for oral proficiency rather than needing to read or write the language. In the early centuries of the empire transliterated Latin-learning papyri are actually more common than ones employing the Roman alphabet, but from the third century the use of the Roman alphabet predominates.

At the elementary level language students used bilingual easy readers, in which everything was given both in the foreign language and in their own language; the Colloquia are prime examples of such texts, but there were also other bilingual texts. Learners then moved on to monolingual texts, which they read with the aid of glossaries and commentaries, and to translating short passages into the language being learned. To help with these tasks they had three kinds of glossaries: most common were classified glossaries arranged by topic, which were used for memorising vocabulary, but when reading an unfamiliar text learners could also use glossaries in alphabetical order or running word-lists compiled for that particular text.

Grammar was taught as well, with the complication that the ancients did not have the idea that the grammar of one language could be described in another language. So grammars of Greek were written exclusively in Greek and grammars of Latin exclusively in Latin; the only exception seems to be the Latin grammar of Dositheus, which was bilingual for the portions students used at the very beginning of their Latin studies but only in Latin for the portions they read later. Paradigms were learned in tables very similar to those used today, except that whereas we would put the framework of a paradigm (the labels indicating which form is which) in the students' own language, the ancients put that framework in the language being learned.

Our evidence for how language study was conducted comes from a variety of sources, including both original ancient documents and texts transmitted via medieval manuscripts. The original documents are papyri, tablets, and ostraca; because the dry climate of Egypt preserves such materials much better than most other parts of the empire the majority of these texts come from Egypt. Since Egypt was Greek-speaking, this accident of preservation means that in certain respects we know more about how Greek speakers (and, in the case of a few documents, Coptic speakers) learned Latin than about how Latin speakers learned Greek. The documents can often be traced to a particular time and place by archaeological context, handwriting, or their re-use of a document bearing a date. Unfortunately they are usually fragmentary and often difficult to decipher, and the total amount of text they contain is not large.

Language-learning texts that survive intact via the manuscript tradition offer a valuable complement to the original documents because they are usually intact and much longer than the documents. The prime examples of such texts are the Hermeneumata Pseudodositheana themselves, but we also have a number of grammatical texts designed for language learners and some bilingual glossaries.

For further information see Kramer (1983 and 2001, collections of bilingual papyri many of which were used for language learning), Bonnet (2005, edition of Dositheus' grammar), Dickey, Ferri, and Scappaticcio (2013, on the ancient use of paradigm tables), and Dickey (2010, on the creation of language-teaching materials; 2012–15: especially 1.4–15; 2015a, an overview of the types of ancient language-teaching materials with examples of each; and 2016, presentation of the ancient language-teaching materials in a format suitable for modern students).

12.5 HOW THE COLLOQUIA WERE USED

Today, language teaching does not normally involve bilingual materials; we tend to think that our students should interact directly with the language they are trying to learn, rather than using a translation as a crutch. Clearly the ancient attitude was very different, because a high percentage of the surviving ancient language-learning materials are fully bilingual. Such materials could not have been used for translation practice, and that raises questions about what users actually did with them.

The phrasebook sections could, of course, have been employed like modern phrasebooks, which users tend to treat as reference works: the buyer of a modern phrasebook normally does not study it in advance, but looks up phrases in it when they are needed. Those portions of the Colloquia that consist of sets of phrases for particular situations could in theory also have been used as reference works, but several considerations suggest that they were not in practice so employed.

In the first place, it is difficult to use even a modern phrasebook effectively enough to communicate in a language the user does not know at all. The particular thing the user needs to say may not be included in the phrasebook, and even if it is included he may not be able to find it within the time limit of his listener's patience. Writers and publishers of modern phrasebooks go to great lengths to tackle both these problems by including as many phrases as possible and by arranging them into clearly-marked sections with colour-coded pages so that users will be able to find what they need as fast as possible, but even with those aids the difficulties of using a phrasebook under pressure are still severe. Ancient phasebooks would have been much harder to use efficiently, because the papyrus-roll format of ancient books and the absence of colour-coding and in many cases even of headings would have made it far more time-consuming to find a specific piece of information. And some of the phrases contained in the ancient phrasebooks, such as the insults, are not amenable to being used directly from a reference work (see introduction to passage 6.3).

The school scenes of the Colloquia contain several references to use of the Hermeneumata and of conversation manuals, and these references usually indicate that the student learns material and then recites it. This memorisation-and-oral-recitation system is in any case to be expected, for it was common in ancient education more generally. The text does not specify whether the material memorised was the Latin half, the Greek half, or both, but probably students memorised the half in the language they were trying to learn and used the half in their native language to make sure they understood what the phrases they memorised meant.

Many sections of the Colloquia contain dialogues between two or more speakers. Nowadays, language students often practise performing similar dialogues with a fellow student; for example if a dialogue involves the purchase of a sandwich in a café, one student may play the part of the customer and the other the part of the waiter. Unfortunately, we have no evidence for how the dialogue passages of the Hermeneumata Colloquia were recited: they may have been performed by several students as in these modern examples, but they may also have been recited as a unit by a single student.

12.6 THE TRANSLATION SYSTEM USED IN THE COLLOQUIA

The Colloquia are composed in a special bilingual format that was common in antiquity but has no parallels in modern usage. The two languages are arranged in narrow parallel columns, one to three words wide (see figure 13); usually the language the student was learning occupies the left-hand column, and the language already known occupies the right-hand column. The line breaks are usually meaningful, marking off units such as a preposition and its object, an adjective and the noun it pertains to, etc. Since word division was not normally used in antiquity, these line divisions by themselves would have made the text substantially easier to understand.

The two languages were further arranged so that the translation of each line in the left-hand column could be found in the corresponding line in the right-hand column. A student who did not understand the words in one column could thus find their meaning immediately by looking in the other column; in that respect the ancient format resembles our interlinear translations, in which it is easy to identify immediately the translation of any word in the original that one does not know. But this 'columnar' translation format, unlike our interlinear translations, also makes clear the overall meaning of the sentence, for one can read down either column to get a fully coherent text.

In fact this 'columnar' translation format has substantial advantages over any of the formats used today in presenting bilingual text. Our interlinear translations tell the reader the meanings of words but not of sentences, our facing-page translations tell the reader the meanings of sentences but not of words, and the various combinations of these two that are sometimes employed (e.g. by linguists needing to make precise arguments that require the reader to understand fully a sentence in a language the reader may never have encountered before) are long and cumbersome. The columnar format, by contrast, is a simple and

ΟΡΘΡΟΥ	ANTELUCEM	BEFOREDAYLIGHT
ΕΓΡΗΓΟΡΗΣΑ	VIGILAVI	IAWOKE
ΕΞΥΠΝΟΥ	DESOMNO	FROMSLEEP
ΑΝΕΣΤΗΝ	SURREXI	IGOTUP
ΕΚΤΗΣΚΛΙΝΗΣ	DELECTO	FROMTHEBED
ΕΚΑΘΙΣΑ	SEDI	ISATDOWN
ΕΛΑΒΟΝ	ACCEPI	ITOOK
ΥΠΟΔΕΣΜΙΔΑΣ	PEDULES	GAITERS
ΚΑΛΙΓΙΑ	CALIGAS	BOOTS
ΥΠΕΔΗΣΑΜΗΝ	CALCIAVIME	IPUTONMYBOOTS
ΗΤΗΣΑ	POPOSCI	IASKEDFOR
ΥΔΩΡ	AQUAM	WATER
ΕΙΣΟΨΙΝ	ADFACIEM	FORMYFACE
ΝΙΠΤΟΜΑΙ	LAVO	IWASH
ΠΡΩΤΟΝΤΑΣΧΕΙΡΑΣ	PRIMOMANUS	MYHANDSFIRST
ΕΙΤΑΤΗΝΟΨΙΝ	DEINDEFACIEM	THENMYFACE
ΕΝΙΨΑΜΗΝ	LAVI	IWASHED
ΑΠΕΜΑΞΑ	EXTERSI	IDRIEDMYSELF
ΑΠΕΘΗΚΑΤΗΝΕΓΚΟΙΜΗΤΡΑΝ	DEPOSUIDORMITORIAM	ITOOKOFFMYNIGHTCLOTHES
ΕΛΑΒΟΝΧΙΤΩΝΑ	ACCEPITUNICAM	ITOOKATUNIC
ΠΡΟΣΤΟΣΩΜΑ	ADCORPUS	FORMYBODY
ΠΕΡΙΕΖΩΣΑΜΗΝ	PRAECINXIME	IPUTONMYBELT
ΗΛΕΙΨΑΤΗΝΚΕΦΑΛΗΝΜΟΥ	UNXICAPUTMEUM	IANOINTEDMYHEAD
ΚΑΙΕΚΤΕΝΙΣΑ	ETPECTINAVI	ANDCOMBEDMYHAIR
ΕΠΟΙΗΣΑΠΕΡΙΤΟΝΤΡΑΧΗΛΟΝ	FECICIRCACOLLUM	IPUTAROUNDMYNECK
ΑΝΑΒΟΛΑΙΟΝ	PALLAM	AMANTLE
ΕΝΕΔΥΣΑΜΗΝ	INDUIME	IPUTON
ΕΠΕΝΔΥΤΗΝ	SUPERARIAM	ANOUTERGARMENT
ΛΕΥΚΗΝΕΠΑΝΩ	ALBAMSUPRA	AWHITEONE(AND)ONTOP
ΕΝΔΥΟΜΑΙΦΕΛΟΝΗΝ	INDUOPAENULAM	IPUTONAHOODEDCAPE
ΠΡΟΗΛΘΟΝ	PROCESSI	IWENTOUT
ΕΚΤΟΥΚΟΙΤΩΝΟΣ	DECUBICULO	OFTHEBEDROOM
ΣΥΝΤΩΠΑΙΔΑΓΩΓΩ	CUMPAEDAGOGO	WITHMYPAEDAGOGUE
ΚΑΙΣΥΝΤΗΤΡΟΦΩ	ETCUMNUTRICE	ANDWITHMYNURSE
ΑΣΠΑΣΑΣΘΑΙ	SALUTARE	TOGREET
ΤΟΝΠΑΤΕΡΑ	PATREM	MYFATHER
ΚΑΙΤΗΝΜΗΤΕΡΑ	ETMATREM	ANDMOTHER
ΑΜΦΟΤΕΡΟΥΣΗΣΠΑΣΑΜΗΝ	AMBOSSALUTAVI	IGREETEDTHEMBOTH
ΚΑΙΚΑΤΕΦΙΛΗΣΑ	ETOSCULATUSSUM	ANDIKISSEDTHEM
ΚΑΙΟΥΤΩΣΚΑΤΑΒΑΙΝΩ	ETSICDESCENDI	ANDTHENICAMEDOWN
ΕΚΤΟΥΟΙΚΟΥ	DEDOMO	FROMTHEHOUSE

FIG. 57 The beginning of passage 2.2 in its original columnar format, with an English translation also using columnar format and with ancient conventions

efficient method of presenting all the necessary information. It is made possible not primarily by the flexibility in word order inherent in both Latin and Greek – the two languages are not so similar that a word-for-word translation can be coherent – but by the writer's ability to choose the size of the units translated. In passages where a word-for-word translation works well, the lines of a columnar translation are frequently only one word long, giving the reader maximum information about which Greek word matches which Latin one. But when

Ὄρθρου	Ante lucem	Before daylight
ἐγρηγόρησα	vigilavi	I awoke
ἐξ ὕπνου·	de somno;	from sleep;
ἀνέστην	surrexi	I got up
ἐκ τῆς κλίνης,	de lecto,	from the bed,
ἐκάθισα,	sedi,	I sat down,
ἔλαβον	accepi	I took
ὑποδεσμίδας,	pedules,	gaiters,
καλίγια·	caligas;	boots;
ὑπεδησάμην·	calciavi me.	I put on my boots.
ᾔτησα	poposci	I asked for
ὕδωρ	aquam	water
εἰς ὄψιν·	ad faciem	for my face;
νίπτομαι	lavo	I wash
πρῶτον τὰς χεῖρας,	primo manus,	my hands first,
εἶτα τὴν ὄψιν	deinde faciem	then my face
ἐνιψάμην·	lavi;	I washed;
ἀπέμαξα.	extersi.	I dried myself.
ἀπέθηκα τὴν ἐγκοιμήτραν·	deposui dormitoriam;	I took off my night-clothes;
ἔλαβον χιτῶνα	accepi tunicam	I took a tunic
πρὸς τὸ σῶμα·	ad corpus;	for my body;
περιεζωσάμην,	praecinxi me;	I put on my belt;
ἤλειψα τὴν κεφαλήν μου	unxi caput meum	I anointed my head
καὶ ἐκτένισα·	et pectinavi;	and combed (my hair);
ἐποίησα περὶ τὸν τράχηλον	feci circa collum	I put around my neck
ἀναβόλαιον·	pallam;	a mantle;
ἐνεδυσάμην	indui me	I put on
ἐπενδύτην	superariam	an outer garment,
λευκήν· ἐπάνω	albam, supra	a white one, (and) on top
ἐνδύομαι φελόνην.	induo paenulam.	I put on a hooded cape.
προῆλθον	processi	I went out
ἐκ τοῦ κοιτῶνος	de cubiculo	of the bedroom
σὺν τῷ παιδαγωγῷ	cum paedagogo	with my paedagogue
καὶ σὺν τῇ τροφῷ	et cum nutrice	and with my nurse,
ἀσπάσασθαι	salutare	to greet
τὸν πατέρα	patrem	my father
καὶ τὴν μητέρα.	et matrem.	and mother.
ἀμφοτέρους ἠσπασάμην	ambos salutavi	I greeted them both
καὶ κατεφίλησα,	et osculatus sum,	and I kissed them,
καὶ οὕτως καταβαίνω	et sic descendi	and then I came down
ἐκ τοῦ οἴκου.	de domo.	from the house.

FIG. 58 The beginning of passage 2.2 in its original columnar format, with an English translation also using columnar format and with modern conventions

a difference of grammar or word order arises, the writer makes a longer line, within which the words can come in a different order in the two languages.

In fact even English, with its largely fixed word order, can be used effectively in the columnar translation format. Figures 57 and 58 provide examples of a passage from the Colloquia (the beginning of passage 2.2 with a more literal English translation) in its original columnar format, with a third column added in English. The text is given first with ancient conventions and then with modern ones.

The bilingual nature of the Colloquia and their distinctive format cannot be preserved in this book, but the original format is worth keeping in mind, as it was central to their conception and purpose. For further information see Dickey (2015b, examination of the history and ancient distribution of the columnar format; 2012–15, Colloquia presented trilingually in this format; 2016, various ancient Latin-teaching materials presented bilingually in this format).

12.7 HISTORY AND TRANSMISSION OF THE COLLOQUIA

As explained in chapter 12.1, the Colloquia are put together from two distinct sources, a single schoolbook composed in the West before the first century AD and one or more phrasebooks composed in the East, probably in the second century. Neither was originally part of the Hermeneumata Pseudodositheana collection, which originally consisted of a preface and glossaries, but the schoolbook was attached to that collection (immediately after the initial preface) in the East in the first or second century. A process of repeated adaptation for use by different teachers in different settings caused the Hermeneumata Pseudodositheana, and therefore the Colloquia, to split into different versions that gradually diverged from one another. That process of divergence probably began in the second century and was well underway by the third century.

The phrasebooks seem to have been attached to the schoolbooks (and hence to the Hermeneumata Pseudodositheana) somewhat later, after the different versions had begun to diverge. Thus one Colloquium (the Colloquium Stephani) lacks a phrasebook entirely, and in another (the Colloquia Monacensia–Einsidlensia) there is evidence that the phrasebook was transmitted separately from the schoolbook as late as the medieval period.

By the late antique period this process of divergence had produced at least eight different versions of the Colloquia; that is, there are eight from which material survives, and it is virtually certain that others also existed and have been lost. Two of those versions were eventually spliced back together to form the Colloquium Celtis, though it is uncertain whether this joining took place in antiquity or afterwards. As a result, that Colloquium has a somewhat peculiar story line in which the main character gets up and dresses repeatedly, goes off to school twice, leaves school three times, and eventually goes to bed twice at the end of the day. Another version, which is known to have existed because a fragment is preserved on papyrus, has been lost apart from that fragment. To all intents and purposes, therefore, there are six surviving Colloquia.

Apart from a few papyrus fragments, the main form in which the Colloquia survive is medieval manuscripts, written between the ninth century and the Renaissance: the texts were copied and recopied over many centuries by different people who wanted them for different purposes. In theory, bilingual texts such as the Colloquia could have survived either via the Eastern (Byzantine) manuscript tradition, which is the way most ancient Greek literature has survived, or via the Western manuscript tradition, which is the way most Latin literature has survived. In practice, however, texts involving Latin very rarely survive via the Eastern tradition, and the Colloquia are no exception: all six surviving Colloquia are preserved only via the Western manuscript tradition. Since all but one of them show clear signs of having circulated in the East in antiquity, this transmission implies that Western Greek teachers eventually re-borrowed teaching materials from the East rather than simply continuing to use the original Western schoolbook and Hermeneumata versions. Such re-borrowing shows the fluid boundaries between East and West during the empire and the ease with which books and information were exchanged; it also suggests that the adaptations made by teachers in the East were attractive to those in the West. The re-borrowing must have taken place before the end of the sixth century, after which conditions in both halves of the Mediterranean would have made it impractical.

During the medieval period the Hermeneumata Pseudodositheana (including the Colloquia) were copied by Western scholars who wanted to use them to learn Greek. It is often said that no-one knew Greek in the medieval West and that the language had to be completely re-introduced in the Renaissance, and there is much truth in that version of events. But what it overlooks is the fact that a significant number of people in the medieval West tried very hard to learn Greek. Most of them did not succeed, but the persistence of their efforts is impressive, and the Hermeneumata played a major role in those efforts.

One reason why most of the medieval scholars who tried to use the Hermeneumata Pseudodositheana to learn Greek were doomed to failure is that the text was not usable on its own without a teacher. The Hermeneumata contained impressive glossaries and, at least in some versions, a large amount of bilingual text that could be used as reading practice, but there was little or nothing in the way of grammar, neither paradigms nor explanations of syntax. Medieval users clearly felt this lack of grammatical information keenly and attempted to supply the deficiency by finding bilingual grammatical materials such as Dositheus' grammar, but their attempts met with little success, because the grammatical materials they found normally pertained to Latin rather than to Greek grammar. Paradigm tables in which the Greek was simply a translation of the Latin provided only very haphazard coverage of the Greek paradigm system, for example providing declensional information only for those nouns that happened to be translations of the paradigms for each Latin declension.

The use of Dositheus' grammar as a means of learning Greek syntax was equally unfortunate, for Dositheus described Latin from the perspective of Greek speakers and therefore concentrated almost exclusively on those features of Latin that are not paralleled in Greek. For example his discussion of case usage ignores the nominative, vocative, accusative, genitive, and dative cases, which are used in Greek, and focusses on the ablative, which Greek does not have.

The other reason why the medieval Hermeneumata manuscripts could not effectively be used to learn Greek is that the Greek in those manuscripts is often seriously corrupt. Copied repeatedly by scribes unfamiliar not only with the Greek language but even with the Greek alphabet, the Greek was severely damaged; in many of the manuscripts it was also transliterated into the Latin alphabet and then had word divisions inserted as if it were actually Latin. The result is a text that modern scholars, with prior knowledge of Greek and enormous resources at their disposal in terms of reference works created since the middle ages, can often only just manage to decipher. For a Greekless twelfth-century scholar it would have been hopeless.

Despite all this, there is evidence that medieval scholars placed great value on the knowledge potentially contained in the Hermeneumata collections. According to monastery records preserved in Austria, early in the twelfth century a group of Cistercian monks set out from a monastery at Morimond in France to found a daughter house in the Austrian mountains. They carried with them the essential books that would be needed to form the spiritual and intellectual nucleus of their new community, including a massive volume containing the Hermeneumata Pseudodositheana. After a long and arduous trek they arrived at what is now Heiligenkreuz and set to work building themselves a magnificent monastery, which still survives as a monument to their hard work and excellent artistic taste.

Until they had completed those monastery buildings, the monks lived in temporary accommodation that was probably unsuited to sustained intellectual endeavour in the rigours of an Austrian winter. But despite the unsuitable accommodation and the pressures of the building works, within a few years the monks had made a copy of the Hermeneumata Pseudodositheana. They had also attracted a substantial number of converts, so many that they determined to send out a second colony to an even more inhospitable set of mountains to their north. These colonists were given the original volumes brought from Morimond to form the nucleus of their own future library, while the Heiligenkreuz community kept the new copies that they had made after arriving from France.

The colonists duly crossed the mountains and founded the monastery of Zwettl, which is also a splendid edifice, and soon after doing so, again probably before the monastery buildings were completed, they took care to make their own new copy of the Hermeneumata Pseudodositheana. Both the Heiligenkreuz and the Zwettl copies come from a particularly corrupt version of the Hermeneumata tradition, with the Greek transliterated and garbled. It seems almost inconceivable that they could have been any use to the monks who copied them, but nevertheless those monks valued them highly and prioritised copying them over other activities that one might have expected to be more urgent.

Although the medieval Hermeneumata manuscripts were mostly unusable as a self-standing Greek course, some of them would have been helpful in combination with a teacher who actually knew Greek. The manuscripts contain evidence that such teachers occasionally appeared (presumably in the form of travellers from the East), for there are occasional alterations revealing the influence of medieval Greek.

In the Renaissance the potential of the Hermeneumata, and especially the Colloquia, as Greek-learning tools was swiftly recognised, and a number of enthusiastic young men embarking on the study of Greek made copies of Hermeneumata manuscripts. When faced with highly corrupt manuscripts these learners often had great difficulty; for example they attempted to re-transliterate transliterated Greek back into the Greek alphabet and often failed miserably. But some managed to find manuscripts where the Greek was in better condition, and for a time the Colloquia were in vogue as a teaching tool. Marsilio Ficino, one of the leading lights of the Italian Renaissance, made a copy of the Hermeneumata early in his study of Greek, as did Conrad Celtes, who lectured on Greek in Vienna. Georges Hermonymus, who taught Greek for decades in Paris and was responsible for introducing many works of Greek literature to France, made several copies of the Colloquia, though he does not appear to have been interested in the rest of the Hermeneumata.

The first printed edition of the Colloquia was produced by Beatus Rhenanus in Basle in 1516, and other publications followed. Of particular importance is that of Stephanus (Henri Estienne) in 1573, as this work preserves two versions of the Colloquia for which the medieval manuscript evidence has been completely or partially lost.

The six surviving Colloquia are named after the manuscripts in which they are found. Therefore they are known as the Colloquia Monacensia–Einsidlensia (after manuscripts in Munich and Einsiedeln Abbey in Switzerland; this version is always named in the plural because it includes two distinct Colloquia, the schoolbook and the phrasebook being separate in the earlier manuscripts), the Colloquium Leidense–Stephani (after a manuscript in Leiden and Stephanus' edition), the Colloquium Stephani (after Stephanus' edition), the Colloquium Harleianum (after a manuscript in the Harley collection of the British Library in London), the Colloquium Montepessulanum (after a manuscript in Montpellier), and the Colloquium Celtis (after a manuscript copied by the Renaissance scholar Conrad Celtes, now preserved in Vienna).

Five of the Colloquia were known to scholars by 1892, when Georg Goetz published his monumental edition of the Hermeneumata Pseudodositheana; this edition consists almost entirely of manuscript transcripts, rather than being a proper edition presenting a corrected text built from multiple sources, but is still the standard edition for most of the Hermeneumata glossaries. (The Leidensia version of the Hermeneumata has received a later edition by Flammini (2004); that text is far more readable than Goetz's but contains numerous errors.) In 1982 Carlotta Dionisotti discovered the Hermeneumata Celtis and published its Colloquium; publication of the glossaries of this version is still in progress, chiefly by Rolando Ferri (e.g. 2011). The only complete edition of the Colloquia, and the only translation, is that of Dickey (2012–15).

For further information see Dionisotti (1982, presenting the discovery of the Colloquium Celtis and summarising the history of the Hermeneumata; 1985, on the history of the Hermeneumata and other glossaries in the early modern period; 1988, on Greek in the Carolingian West), Herren (1988, a collection of pieces on Greek in the medieval West), Kaczynski (1988, on Greek in the medieval West), Berschin (1988, on Greek in the medieval West), and Dickey (2012–15: see the introductions to particular Colloquia for the transmission histories of those Colloquia, and 11.269–99 for the papyri, which have largely been published piecemeal).

12.8 OTHER COLLOQUIA

The ancient Colloquia have been the source and/or the inspiration for numerous similar works composed at later periods. Some of these are based closely on the ancient text, such as the Colloquia produced in the late fifteenth century by Johannes Reuchlin, which can be shown to derive from the Einsidlensia version of the Hermeneumata Pseudodositheana. Others are more tangentially related, such as some of the dialogues of Erasmus.

In some parts of medieval Europe knowledge of Greek was not desired, but the potential of the Colloquia as a Latin-learning tool was nevertheless appreciated. The Greek was therefore either removed, leaving monolingual Latin Colloquia, or replaced with a vernacular language, leaving bilingual texts in a different pair of languages, and the result was used to learn Latin. Such Colloquia were significantly adapted over time and often ceased to have any wording in common with the ancient versions, but they are extremely interesting for the insight they provide into daily life in the early middle ages.

The Colloquium format continued to be used to teach Latin as long as Latin remained useful as a spoken language, so there are numerous post-Renaissance Latin textbooks using it – though it is unclear whether all their authors were aware that the format has ancient roots.

For further information see Gwara and Porter (1997, editions and translations of very cute Latin-only Colloquia from Anglo-Saxon England), Garmonsway (1978, edition of a Colloquium in Latin and Anglo-Saxon), Gwara (1996, edition of Latin Colloquia from tenth-century Britain), Lendinara (1999: 207–87, discussion of the tenth-century Latin Colloquia), Halkin, Bierlaire, and Hoven (1972, edition of Erasmus' Latin Colloquia), and Streckenbach (1970 and 1972, edition, translation, and discussion of Latin Colloquia from fifteenth-century Germany).

Appendix
A School Whipping at Pompeii?

A scene from a Pompeiian wall painting, commonly reproduced in works on ancient education, is usually thought to represent an outdoor school, with three pupils reading on the left and a fourth being whipped on the right (e.g. Bonner 1977: 117–18). Recently, however, it has been suggested that this identification is incorrect and that the person being whipped is an adult slave, not a schoolboy (Selinger 2001: 350–4); because of these doubts I have not included the image in chapter 2.

There are two points in favour of the new interpretation. First, the person being whipped does not look like a child: he has the size and proportions of an adult. Of course some boys continued to study once they were the size of an adult, but these advanced students were not whipped freely like younger pupils: Quintilian, whose writings are roughly contemporary with this painting, takes for granted that teachers could beat only little boys and would have to stop when the children grew bigger (*Institutio Oratoria* 1.3.15; cf. Cribiore 1996: 24). Second, school punishments were private chastisements designed to help boys of good family turn into respected citizens, not public humiliations that would continue to embarrass them in adulthood: the mortification entailed by stripping someone almost completely naked and beating him severely in the forum is out of keeping with the way the dignity of Roman citizens was normally protected (Selinger 2001: 351–2).

The fact that the whipping takes place next to people who are apparently reading does not, in itself, show that the two activities are connected, for the painting in question was not originally a self-standing picture but part of a long frieze showing activities in a forum. This frieze decorated the atrium of the estate of Julia Felix at Pompeii; seventeen other fragments of it can be identified today (see Olivito 2013). The forum frieze is strikingly different from most Pompeiian wall painting, not only because of its non-mythological

FIG. 59   Engraving from plate XLI (p. 213) of Anonymous (1762)

subject matter but also because of its 'popular' style, i.e. rough, impressionistic painting, unnatural proportions, and distinctive colour scheme (Ling 1991: 163–5; Maiuri 1953: 139–48). It immediately attracted the attention of the early excavators, with the result that in 1755 most of the frieze was removed from the wall and cut into pieces, not all of which have survived. This eighteenth-century division is what makes the whipping look as if it should be associated with the seated figures: in the original continuous format the whipping might have been simply the next scene in a series of unconnected activities.

The difficulty of understanding this image has been compounded by the fact that soon after the forum frieze was removed from the wall splendid engravings were done of each segment. These engravings are works of art in their own right, and in keeping with eighteenth-century taste they alter the 'popular', impressionistic painting style of the original frieze to a style much closer to that of other Pompeiian wall paintings, full of precise detail and with more naturalistic proportions (e.g. one fragment depicts a mule, which in the original painting has fantastically long legs but in the engraving has normal ones: see Olivito

2013: 38 and cf. Maiuri 1953: 141–3). Because the engravings are so much clearer and more detailed than the originals, they are consistently reproduced instead of photographs of the original painting by scholars interested in the content of the frieze, even when those scholars otherwise prefer photographs to drawings (e.g. Beard 2008: 77). Indeed the preference for the engraving of this scene is so widespread that some unwary writers even claim that the original has been lost (e.g. Bloomer 2015b: 187).

The original is not lost; it is on display in the National Archaeological Museum in Naples (inv. 9066) and is reproduced in a few works on Pompeiian wall painting (e.g. Olivito 2013: 63; Pugliese Carratelli 1991: 255). Many of the scholars who have worked on this image are aware of the differences between the original and the engraving, but they use the engraving anyway, on the grounds that it is more accurate due to the decay of the original painting since the engraving was done (e.g. Olivito 2013: 8; Selinger 2001: 346–7). The problem with this argument is that the engraving is our main piece of evidence for the deterioration of the original, and yet because of its addition of precise detail the engraving does not accurately reflect the eighteenth-century state of the painting.

The engraving shows a shadowy figure on the far right of the scene; the description accompanying the first publication of the engraving (Anonymous 1762: 207–9; this description must be based on examination of the painting itself as well as of the engraving, because it describes colours) states that this figure is partly lost. Recently Olivito (2013: 62–5), re-examining the painting, has argued that the traces in question do not belong to a human figure at all, but to a tall lectern. If Olivito is right, the engraving should not be trusted in any respect – but, nevertheless, if there is a lectern at the far right of the scene the whipping is probably associated with the reading.

Several differences of detail between the engraving and the painting are crucial for determining whether the person being whipped is a schoolboy or a slave. In the engraving the person being whipped looks young, but the details that make him seem youthful are not now visible in the painting: were they ever there? In the painting there is a large dark patch on his lower face, one that looks very much like a beard; in the engraving that dark patch is resolved into an open mouth and some shading. Did the person who designed the engraving see that dark patch more clearly than we do and know that it was not a beard, or did he interpret it in the light of his overall understanding of the scene? How did he come to that understanding: by seeing a clearer version of the painting, or from his own assumptions about what might happen in a forum – is it relevant that in eighteenth-century Naples a person being beaten was far more likely to be a schoolboy than a slave?

In the engraving the person being beaten is shorter than in the painting: the person holding him up has been moved to the right by the engraver, so that instead of standing midway between the man with the whip and the man behind the pillar, he is much closer to the man with the whip. This move must be deliberate and cannot be accounted for by any deterioration of the original: why was it done? To make the proportions more naturalistic? To produce a more aesthetically pleasing composition (this must be the reason why the engraver has also raised the height of the columns in the colonnade, so that the garlands are well above the raised whip)? Or to make the recipient of the punishment look smaller and younger?

These are not questions I am qualified to answer: the interpretation of this scene needs to be completely re-examined by someone with a background in Roman painting and its eighteenth-century treatment. But Selinger's theory raises enough doubts that, in my view, this image should not be used as a representation of a school whipping until such a re-examination has taken place.

Selinger also expresses doubts about the identification of the left-hand side of the picture as an outdoor school (2001: 351), and again the doubts are worth taking seriously. The three seated figures do not look like children; they are as tall as the man standing at the left, who according to the traditional interpretation ought to be their teacher. And while some schooling was indeed conducted outside, that was normally elementary education: if the seated figures are pupils in an outdoor school, they should be visibly children (Bonner 1977: 116–17; Della Corte 1959; Cribiore 1996: 18). Moreover, an outdoor setting was normally connected with a lack of seats, hence the term *chamaididas-kalos* 'teacher on the ground'; indoors, a teacher would normally have a chair, with the pupils sitting on the floor or on benches to study and then standing in front of him to recite (Cribiore 1996: 13–14; Bonner 1977: 128). In this scene it is the 'pupils' who sit on the only available furniture, while the 'teacher' stands. The objects on the laps of the seated figures do not look like either tablets or rolls and are not being held in their hands as was usual for reading materials (compare figure 16). And while in the engraving the man standing at the left has a beard and looks much older than the seated figures, it is uncertain whether the same is true in the original: the presence of the beard in the painting is not only doubtful now, but was already uncertain in the nineteenth century (cf. Helbig 1868: 363). For these reasons the entire scene, not only the whipping, should be treated with caution until a full re-examination has taken place.

Bibliography

Adams, J. N. (2003) *Bilingualism and the Latin Language*. Cambridge.

Andreau, J. (1999) *Banking and Business in the Roman World* (trans. J. Lloyd). Cambridge.

Anonymous (1762) *Le Pitture Antiche d'Ercolano* III (part III of the series Antichità di Ercolano, 1755–92). Naples.

Bagnall, R. (ed.) (2009) *Oxford Handbook of Papyrology*. Oxford.

Baldwin, B. (1983) *The Philogelos or Laughter-lover*. Amsterdam.

Beard, M. (2008) *Pompeii: The Life of a Roman Town*. London.

Berschin, W. (1988) *Greek Letters and the Latin Middle Ages: From Jerome to Nicholas of Cusa* (revised edition translated by J. C. Frakes). Washington, D.C.

Birks, P., and McLeod, G. (1987) *Justinian's Institutes*. London.

Bloomer, W. M. (ed.) (2015a) *A Companion to Ancient Education*. Chichester.

(2015b) 'Corporal Punishment in the Ancient School', in Bloomer (2015a) 184–98.

Bonner, S. F. (1977) *Education in Ancient Rome: From the Elder Cato to the Younger Pliny*. London.

Bonnet, G. (2005) *Dosithée: Grammaire latine*. Paris.

Bowman, A. K. (2003) *Life and Letters on the Roman Frontier: Vindolanda and its People* (rev. edn). London.

Calza, G. (1923) 'Le origini latine dell'abitazione moderna', *Architettura e Arti Decorative* 3: 3–18, 49–62.

Cool, H. E. M. (2006) *Eating and Drinking in Roman Britain*. Cambridge.

Cooley, A. E., and Cooley, M. G. L. (2014) *Pompeii and Herculaneum: A Sourcebook* (2nd edn). London.

Cribiore, R. (1996) *Writing, Teachers, and Students in Graeco-Roman Egypt*. Atlanta.

(2001) *Gymnastics of the Mind: Greek Education in Hellenistic and Roman Egypt*. Princeton.

(2007) *The School of Libanius in Late Antique Antioch*. Princeton.

Cribiore, R., Davoli, P., and Ratzan, D. M. (2008) 'A Teacher's Dipinto from Trimithis (Dakhleh Oasis)', *Journal of Roman Archaeology* 21: 170–91.

Dalby, A. R. (2003) *Food in the Ancient World, from A to Z.* London.

Della Corte, M. (1959) 'Scuole e maestri in Pompei antica', *Studi Romani* 7: 621–34.

Derda, T., Markiewicz, T., and Wipszycka, E. (edd.) (2007) *Alexandria: Auditoria of Kom El-Dikka and Late Antique Education.* Warsaw.

Dickey, E. (2010) 'The Creation of Latin Teaching Materials in Antiquity: A Re-interpretation of P.Sorb. inv. 2069', *Zeitschrift für Papyrologie und Epigraphik* 175: 188–208.

(2012–15) *The Colloquia of the Hermeneumata Pseudodositheana.* Cambridge.

(2015a) 'Teaching Latin to Greek Speakers in Antiquity', in E. P. Archibald, W. Brockliss, and J. Gnoza (edd.), *Learning Latin and Greek from Antiquity to the Present* (Cambridge) 30–51.

(2015b) 'Columnar Translation: An Ancient Interpretive Tool that the Romans Gave the Greeks', *Classical Quarterly* 65: 807–21.

(2016) *Learning Latin the Ancient Way.* Cambridge.

Dickey, E., Ferri, R., and Scappaticcio, M. C. (2013) 'The Origins of Grammatical Tables: A Reconsideration of P.Louvre inv. E 7332', *Zeitschrift für Papyrologie und Epigraphik* 187: 173–89.

Dionisotti, A. C. (1982) 'From Ausonius' Schooldays? A Schoolbook and its Relatives', *Journal of Roman Studies* 72: 83–125.

(1985) 'From Stephanus to Du Cange: Glossary Stories', *Revue d'Histoire des Textes* 14–15:303–36.

(1988) 'Greek Grammars and Dictionaries in Carolingian Europe', in Herren (1988) 1–56.

Dunbabin, K. M. D. (2003) *The Roman Banquet: Images of Conviviality.* Cambridge.

Fagan, G. G. (1999) *Bathing in Public in the Roman World.* Ann Arbor.

Ferri, R. (2011) '*Hermeneumata Celtis*: The Making of a Late-antique Bilingual Glossary', in R. Ferri (ed.), *The Latin of Roman Lexicography* (Pisa) 141–69.

Fitzgerald, J. T. (ed.) (1997) *Greco-Roman Perspectives on Friendship.* Atlanta.

Flammini, G. (2004) *Hermeneumata Pseudodositheana Leidensia.* Munich.

Garmonsway (1978) *Aelfric's Colloquy* (3rd edn). Exeter.

Goetz, G. (1892) *Hermeneumata Pseudodositheana* (vol. III of *Corpus Glossariorum Latinorum*). Leipzig.

Gordon, W. M., and Seckel, E. (1988) *The Institutes of Gaius.* London.

Graser, E. R. (1940) 'The Edict of Diocletian on Maximum Prices', in T. Frank, *An Economic Survey of Ancient Rome* v: *Rome and Italy of the Empire* (Baltimore) 305–421.

Grocock, C., and Grainger, S. (2006) *Apicius.* Totnes.

Gwara, S. (1996) *Latin Colloquies from Pre-conquest Britain.* Toronto.

Gwara, S., and Porter, D. W. (1997) *Anglo-Saxon Conversations: The Colloquies of Ælfric Bata*. Woodbridge.

Halkin, L.-E., Bierlaire, F., and Hoven, R. (1972) *Opera Omnia Desiderii Erasmi Roterodami* 1.111: *Colloquia*. Amsterdam.

Harris, W. V. (2006) 'A Revisionist View of Roman Money', *Journal of Roman Studies* 96: 1–24.

Helbig, W. (1868) *Wandgemälde der vom Vesuv verschütteten Städte Campaniens*. Leipzig.

Herren, M. W. (ed.) (1988) *The Sacred Nectar of the Greeks: The Study of Greek in the West in the Early Middle Ages*. London.

Holleran, C. (2012) *Shopping in Ancient Rome: The Retail Trade in the Late Republic and the Principate*. Oxford.

Jones, D. (2006) *The Bankers of Puteoli: Finance, Trade, and Industry in the Roman World*. Stroud.

Joyal, M., McDougall, I., and Yardley, J. C. (2009) *Greek and Roman Education: A Sourcebook*. London.

Kaczynski, B. M. (1988) *Greek in the Carolingian Age: The St. Gall Manuscripts*. Cambridge, Mass.

Konstan, D. (1997) *Friendship in the Classical World*. Cambridge.

Kramer, J. (1983) *Glossaria Bilinguia in Papyris et Membranis Reperta*. Bonn. (2001) *Glossaria Bilinguia Altera*. Munich.

Lendinara, P. (1999) *Anglo-Saxon Glosses and Glossaries*. Aldershot.

Ling, R. (1991) *Roman Painting*. Cambridge.

Maiuri, A. (1953) *Roman Painting*. Geneva.

Morgan, T. (1998) *Literate Education in the Hellenistic and Roman Worlds*. Cambridge.

Mullen, A. (2013) *Southern Gaul and the Mediterranean: Multilingualism and Multiple Identities in the Iron Age and Roman Periods*. Cambridge.

Mullen, A., and James, P. (edd.) (2012) *Multilingualism in the Graeco-Roman Worlds*. Cambridge.

Nielsen, I. (1990) *Thermae et Balnea: The Architecture and Cultural History of Roman Public Baths* (trans. P. Crabb). Aarhus.

Olivito, R. (2013) *Il foro nell'atrio: immagini di architetture, scene di vita e di mercato nel fregio dai Praedia di Iulia Felix (Pompei, 11, 4, 3)*. Bari.

Parsons, P. (2007) *City of the Sharp-nosed Fish: Greek Lives in Roman Egypt*. London.

Pugliese Carratelli, G. (1991) *Pompei: Pitture e Mosaici* 111. Rome.

Rochette, B. (1997) *Le latin dans le monde grec: recherches sur la diffusion de la langue et des lettres latines dans les provinces hellénophones de l'Empire romain*. Brussels.

(1998) 'Le bilinguisme gréco-latin et la question des langues dans le monde gréco-romain: chronique bibliographique', *Revue Belge de Philologie et d'Histoire* 76.1: 177–96.

(2008) 'L'enseignement du latin comme L² dans la *Pars Orientis* de l'empire romain: les *Hermeneumata pseudo-dositheana*', in F. Bellandi and R. Ferri (edd.), *Aspetti della scuola nel mondo romano* (Amsterdam) 81–109.

Roller, M. B. (2006) *Dining Posture in Ancient Rome: Bodies, Values, and Status*. Princeton.

Russell, D. A. (2001) *Quintilian: The Orator's Education, Books 1–2.* Cambridge, Mass.

Salza Prina Ricotti, E. (1995) *Dining as a Roman Emperor: How to Cook Ancient Roman Recipes Today*. Rome.

Selinger, R. (2001) 'Das Recht im Bild: die Forumsszenen der praedia Iuliae Felicis (regio 11, insula 4, domus 3)', *Zeitschrift der Savigny-Stiftung für Rechtsgeschichte: Romanistische Abteilung* 118: 344–64.

Shackleton Bailey, D. R. (1993) *Martial: Epigrams*. Cambridge, Mass.

Slater, W. J. (ed.) (1991) *Dining in a Classical Context*. Ann Arbor.

Streckenbach, G. (1970) 'Paulus Niavis, "Latinum ydeoma pro novellis studentibus": ein Gesprächbüchlein aus dem letzten Viertel des 15. Jahrhunderts', *Mittellateinisches Jahrbuch* 6: 152–91.

(1972) 'Paulus Niavis, "Latinum ydeoma pro novellis studentibus": ein Gesprächbüchlein aus dem letzten Viertel des 15. Jahrhunderts 11', *Mittellateinisches Jahrbuch* 7: 187–251.

Thurmond, D. L. (2006) *A Handbook of Food Processing in Classical Rome*. Leiden.

von Reden, S. (2010) *Money in Classical Antiquity*. Cambridge.

(2012) 'Money and Finance', in W. Scheidel (ed.), *The Cambridge Companion to the Roman Economy* (Cambridge) 266–86.

Williams, C. A. (2012) *Reading Roman Friendship*. Cambridge.

Yegül, F. (1992) *Baths and Bathing in Classical Antiquity*. New York.

(2010) *Bathing in the Roman World*. Cambridge.